Oslo

Front cover: Norway's
Parliament building
Right: Carved animal head at
the Viking Ship Museum

TOP 10 ATTRACTIONS

Akershus Fortress and Castle. They have presided regally over Oslo's inner harbour for centuries. See page 42.

Norwegian Folk Museum. Get a feel for the country's rich cultural heritage. See page 50.

Ibsen Museum. Pay homage to the literary giant. See page 33.

Fram Museum. One of three museums on the Bygdøy Peninsula highlighting Norway's maritime heritage. See page 51.

Viking Ship Museum. Visit some of Norway's most important national treasures. See page 48.

Opera House. Walk around, and even on top of, Oslo's waterfront landmark. See page 83.

Frogner Park. Stroll, play, picnic and admire the statues of prolific sculptor Gustav Vigeland. See page 58.

Nobel Peace Center. A showcase for the Nobel Peace Prize. See page 46.

Marka. Walk, hike, cycle, paddle or ski in the inviting hills and forests surrounding the city. See page 69.

Munch Museum. Dedicated to the life and works of Norwegian artist Edvard Munch. See page 64.

A PERFECT DAY

9.00am Breakfast

Get the day off to a thoroughly Norwegian start with a buffet breakfast at your hotel. It's bound to include salmon and pickled herrings. If that's not your style, head for a coffee in the sedate and sophisticated surrounds of the Grand Café.

12 noon Inner harbour

After a quick T-bane ride back into the centre, visit City Hall, poke around the shops of Aker Brygge and visit the avant-garde art and architecture of the Astrup Fearnley Museum. Lunch at Solsiden, if you are visiting between May and September. Otherwise, try Café Skansen or Kaffistova.

2.00pm Museums

After lunch, jump on a ferry bound for the Bygdøy peninsula where the four museums – the Norwegian Folk Museum, Viking Ship Museum, Polar Ship Fram and Kon-Tiki Museum – provide a fascinating stroll through Norway's history and the city's pioneering spirit.

10.00am Opera & Munch

To catch the essence of this harbourside city's personality, wander down to the waterfront and climb the roof of the daringly designed Opera House. After enjoying the views and architecture, catch a T-bane train out to the Munch Museum, artistic home to many masterpieces by Edvard Munch: the earlier in the day you go the better because crowds can be overwhelming as the day goes on.

IN OSLO

5.30pm Grünerløkka

As locals finish work, a good many of them gravitate towards Grünerløkka, the vaguely alternative early-evening haunt for Oslo's artsy and professional crowd. Soak up the bar atmosphere, window shop and then have dinner at SüdØst, which is this funky neighbourhood in microcosm.

10.00pm On the town

After a taxi back into the city centre, you will have some choices to make. Those looking for a quiet end to the night should consider the atmospheric Fridtjof, followed by last drinks at Dagligstuen. If, however, you are keen to dance your way towards dawn, then it simply has to be Smuget, Onkel Donald or Last Train.

4.00pm City stroll

A ferry ride back to the main harbour allows you to appreciate the beauty of Oslo from the fjord. Then it is time for a stroll the length of Karl Johans Gate, all the way up to the Royal Palace, with some time built in for shopping on the way back.

7.30pm Cocktails

If you're enjoying the Grünerløkka vibe, join the crowds at Kaos or sit back and sip cocktails at Fru Hagen, one of those places where Oslo's love affair with Grünerløkka began. Olympen is another excellent choice among many.

CONTENTS

INTRODUCTION

Norway's energetic capital sits at the top of its own horse-shoe-shaped fjord, relishing its role as the well-endowed gateway to a stunningly beautiful country. The Oslo Fjord juts into southeastern Norway from the waters that join the Baltic to the North Sea, and a cruise or ferry up the fjord from, for example, Copenhagen, is a spectacular way to approach this oldest of Scandinavian capitals.

A Prosperous Capital

Whichever way you arrive, the signs of Oslo's prosperity are apparent at once, from the new Mercedes and Volvos in the taxi fleet to the construction cranes that constantly reshape the city's landscape. It was not always like this. Oslo was the capital of one of Europe's most disadvantaged countries until the discovery of offshore oil in 1969. The resulting transformation was dramatic and today Norway ranks as one of the world's largest oil exporters – not bad for a small country of just 5 million people on the northern fringe of Europe.

Its capital, along with the rest of the country, enjoyed prosperity when oil prices soared. Oil revenues led to low unemployment and a windfall for a state treasury that nevertheless continues to tax its citizens (and visitors) heavily. While a significant proportion of the revenues is locked away in a fund for future generations, the unmistakeable affluence of Norwegians and an easing of strict government controls have clearly revolutionised what was once considered one of Europe's dullest and most expensive capitals.

Much of that stigma could be linked to the very government policies that guided the rebuilding of Norway

Frogner Park

after World War II. Years of Labour Party domination yielded principles that no one should be too rich or too poor, giving rise to a modern social welfare state based on strict government regulation and taxation. The system drove up prices on everything from cola to cars, which were among the items that were still rationed, years after the war ended.

It wasn't too long ago that state law forced Oslo stores to close by 5pm, cafés couldn't serve cocktails unless the customer ordered food as well, and eating out was something done only on special occasions. Buying beer, wine, cosmetics or other so-called 'luxury' or 'unnecessary' items remains an expensive affair, but wine with dinner is no longer something reserved for weekends. Gradual political liberalisation, especially in the 1980s, relaxed many of the old rules and Oslo's inhabitants have spent the years since then making up for lost time. With oil-driven affluence spreading through the population and fuelling consumer demand, Oslo has evolved into a vibrant city packed with museums, galleries, shops and an astonishing assortment of bars and restaurants, given its small population. All of this complements a bounty of well-preserved historic sites and the local scenic beauty of the fjord, surrounding hills and forests.

Big City, Small Town

With 613,000 inhabitants, Oslo still mixes the attributes of a big city with the comfort of a town. Its residential neighbourhoods feature an abundance of trees and gardens, making them seem suburban when many are in fact within walking distance of the city centre. Walking is indeed a great way to get around town, with broad pavements, a compact centre and key streets set aside as pedestrian malls.

Despite its compact central area, the city sprawls over more than 450 sq km (170 sq miles), and its highest point is actually deep within a local forest that falls within its boundaries. Its important oil and shipping industries make it an international business centre, but most Oslo residents still tend to downplay their position in the world and think of themselves as fairly provincial. Oslo is cold and dark in the winter, but can be warm in the summer, with seemingly endless daylight and skies that never go black.

The city is divided into east and west by the Aker River, which also continues to be seen as the boundary between working-class districts in the east and upper class

The Grand Hotel

neighbourhoods in the west, although visitors probably will not see much difference.

Growing Internationalism

As Norway's capital Oslo has an active diplomatic community, with embassies and ambassadors' residences dotting the tree-lined streets. A growing multicultural society is nurturing the development of ethnic neighbourhoods and a new sense of internationalism. Traditional Norwegian bakeries now exist alongside Turkish fruit and vegetable stands, Pakistani sweet shops, and sushi bars.

Oslo continues to lure Norwegians from all over the country, and their distinctive dialects mingle with the local ones. The University of Oslo and a host of other specialised schools

Norway and the Nobel Prize

The capital grabs the world's attention once a year when the Oslo-based Norwegian Nobel Committee announces the winner of the Nobel Peace Prize. Swedish industrialist Alfred Nobel earmarked the bulk of his fortune for the creation of the coveted Nobel Prizes, and his will stipulated that while most of the prizes would be awarded in his native Sweden, he wanted the Norwegians to award the most prestigious of them all. It is unclear why, but Norway was still in its uneasy union with Sweden when Nobel died, and some suggest Nobel wanted to give Norway some support. A committee appointed by the Norwegian Parliament selects the winner, announcing its choice in October after sorting through scores of nominations. The prize itself is awarded in Oslo on 10 December, the anniversary of Nobel's death.

As home to the Peace Prize, Oslo plays a visible role in promoting world peace, and Norwegians take the role seriously. The Nobel Peace Center, next to City Hall where the award ceremony occurs, has emerged as an important venue for showcasing peacemaking efforts.

The pride of Oslo, Akershus Fortress and Castle

and colleges form the basis of a large student population, and many of the students remain in Oslo to work. Stavanger, in Norway's southwest, is considered Norway's 'Oil Capital', but Oslo is its financial and economic hub.

The Weather and the Great Outdoors

Oslo's four distinct seasons impact significantly upon the daily lives and lifestyles of the city's inhabitants, but no matter what the season, activity abounds. The vast majority of Norwegians have a great love of the outdoors and do not let the weather get in the way of recreation. They even have a saying for it, which when roughly translated means: 'There's no such thing as bad weather, only bad clothing'. With that in mind, locals and visitors alike are expected to head outdoors, rain or shine. Sturdy walking shoes are important.

Hills and forests surround Oslo on one side, the fjord on the other. Oslo residents and visitors can escape the city in

Forests and fjord offer peaceful breaks from the city's bustle

minutes for the solitude of hiking up a spruce-studded hilltop, sailing on the fjord, or skiing over a frozen lake.

Late autumn and winter are indeed dark, with as little as five hours of daylight a day, but the snow that usually falls by late November lightens up the landscape. Norwegians are masters at making things cosy, from the lit torches placed outside restaurants and shops, to the crackling fireplaces and hordes of candles used inside. Outdoor ice-skating rinks are floodlit (there is one in the heart of the city), as are the parks and ski trails in the hills and forests around the city. Those same hills and forests abound with lakes and marked paths that attract cyclists, hikers, and water sports in the summer.

No matter what time of year a visitor comes to Oslo, a warm welcome can be expected. Norwegians may be modest, even self-deprecating at times, but most are also fiercely patriotic, proud of their Viking heritage and their city, and flattered by the slightest sign of a visitor's interest.

A BRIEF HISTORY

Oslo's history has helped to breed a fierce independence and patriotism among today's residents. This is, after all, the capital of a land that changed from a great Viking power to a dominated territory, before finally re-emerging as an independent nation in its own right. That independence was hard-won, and the Norwegians are not about to take it for granted.

Founded on the Fjord

Oslo itself got off to a relatively modest start a little over 1,000 years ago. By that time, the area at the top of what was later called the Oslo Fjord had already seen centuries of settlements, as far back as the Iron Age. There is evidence that by AD 900, villages had started appearing in the innermost corner of the fjord, east of today's city centre. People also lived and worked in the valley northeast of the villages, mostly on farms carved into the forests on the west, east and north sides of the fjord.

Oslo was founded around AD 1000, at the end of the Viking Age. The main Viking ports were then in the Trondheim area in northern Norway and in Vestfold, south of Oslo. Some historians contend that the settlement's name derives from that of a foreign-born Viking wife. Others claim that it stems from an ancient local farm

A panel of Norse god Thor and his chariot in the City Hall

called 'Ansurlo'. It may also be a compound word built on the old form of the Norwegian word for a hill (*ås*) and the old word for a field, *lo* ('the field below the hill'). Others think 'Os' refers to an ancient Norse god; 'Oslo' would thus mean 'the god's fields'.

It was, at any rate, the name attached to the settlement that started expanding in earnest from around 1050. That is when the Viking king Harald Hardråde built a royal farm near the eastern harbour area now known as Sørenga. The king, bishops, priests and nuns (Oslo and the rest of Norway were Catholic at the time) built several churches and cloisters. Church ruins can be seen today at Middelalderparken (the Middle Ages Park), which the city renewed in the 1990s.

A set of timber piers near the royal compound jutted into the fjord to accommodate the ships used for trade, fishing and, not least, war. Dense clusters of timber homes with low ceilings also sprung up in the area, but Oslo remained fairly small. Both Bergen, a Hanseatic trading port, and Trondheim, home of the Nidaros Cathedral, were bigger and more important than Oslo during the early Middle Ages. It is believed that around 3,000 people lived in Oslo during the 1200s, including craftsmen and traders.

On the rocks

Ancient rock drawings can be found in Oslo, which depict daily life in Scandinavia's earliest settlements. The drawings (*helleratninger*) date from around 1000 BC. Some of those discovered in Oslo are etched into rocks just outside the old Seaman's School (*Sjømannsskole*) on the No. 18 and 19 tramlines east of the centre at Ekeberg.

Devastating Black Death

The 13th century was a time of unrest in Norway, with a series of civil wars and conflicts over royal power. Håkon V Magnusson, who reigned from 1299 until his death in 1319, nonetheless

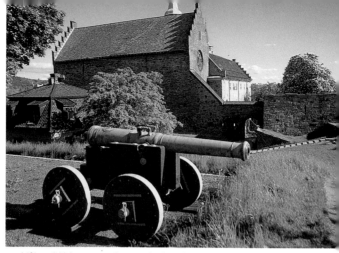

Håkon V Magnusson began the building of Akershus Fortress

started building the stately Akershus Fortress and Castle. He sited it on a point of land across the harbour from the area of Oslo's initial settlements at Bjørvika, now the site of Oslo's Opera House. Håkon V took up permanent residence at Akershus, the first king to do so. Oslo gradually had become an administrative centre for southeastern Norway, and by 1319 it was Norway's capital.

Unrest continued, not least between the local population and early immigrants to Oslo from Rostock. Increasing trade and foreign contact also brought the plague to Norway, and the Black Death *(Svartedauen)* nearly wiped out Oslo's population by 1350. Oslo was devastated, as was the rest of the country. Most of the royal family, the clergy and the merchants succumbed to the plague. Entire villages were depopulated. Farms were idle and the ravages of the disease set off a long period of decline for Norway that lasted through the 15th century.

Decline opened the door for forced unions with other Nordic countries, and Norway wound up as a Danish province in 1536. Then came the Reformation, during which the country became Protestant, removing the power of the Church and leaving cloisters and other Church property to fall into ruin.

A succession of Danish kings moved the city centre to the fortress and castle at Akershus, which in turn led to more building west of the compound in the area called Pipervika. This area today is the site of Oslo's main inner harbour, flanked by City Hall in the heart of town. It remained a backwater of sorts in the late 1500s, with fishermen, workers and soldiers moving in and setting up dense settlements that were subject to disease and fires.

Oslo's cathedral was built during the 17th century

Oslo Becomes 'Christiania'

By 1600, Oslo's economy was picking up, driven by the invention of the sawmill, which greatly increased the value of Norway's vast reserves of timber. Oslo could now produce the boards and planks that Europe needed, and shipbuilding surged. Other natural Norwegian resources, including granite and a variety of minerals, also proved popular.

In 1591 Christian IV became king of Denmark. He took a keen interest in Norway, and especially Oslo, often travelling north. When yet another fire destroyed much of the city in 1624, he decreed that all new buildings must be built of stone, not wood, and that they should be centred behind the walls of Akershus Fortress. This gave rise to the grid-like district called Kvadraturen, where many buildings from the early and mid-1600s still stand. Christian IV took it upon himself to rename Oslo, humbly naming it after himself. From 1624, Oslo became Christiania.

The 1600s saw the construction of new churches, including Vår Frelsers (Our Saviour's), which became Oslo Cathedral (Domkirken), completed in 1698. More Norwegians moved from rural districts to the city, and housing shortages soon arose, along with huge disparities between rich and poor. Some of the old harbour at Bjørvika was filled in to provide more land, while poor settlements sprung up outside the city limits.

Rising Nationalism

By the late 1700s, feelings of nationalism and romanticism over Norway's heritage were taking root across the country, not least in Christiania. Leading patriots had been fighting hard for more autonomy from Denmark and for national institutions of their own. Norway was finally allowed to build its own university in 1811 in Christiania. Before then, students had had to travel to Copenhagen for any advanced learning.

In the early 1800s Christiania found itself cut off from Denmark by British blockades during the Napoleonic Wars. Denmark had sided with France, and the blockades left Norway isolated, but also relatively free from Copenhagen's administration. British victory had profound consequences for Norway, with Denmark having to give up its hold on

Statue of King Carl Johan outside the Royal Palace

the country. The 'founding fathers' of a modern Norway saw their chance, got together at an estate in Eidsvoll north of Christiania, and wrote Norway's constitution. It was finally agreed in 1814 on 17 May, which remains the biggest holiday of the year apart from Christmas.

The signing of the constitution gave most Norwegians a new sense of pride and independence, even though post-war negotiations left Norway in an unhappy union with Sweden for the next 91 years. While hard economic times in rural areas spurred emigration to America, thousands of others simply migrated to Christiania. All were in search of employment, and many lived in crowded conditions.

Christiania's population soared from 30,000 in the early 1800s to 220,000 by 1900. The new constitution confirmed the city's role as a modern national capital, given its history as an administrative centre. With that came the need for new government buildings and, not least, the Parliament

(Stortinget), which was completed in 1866. New national institutions rose in the early 1800s, including the Central Bank (Norges Bank) in 1816, the Stock Exchange (Børsen) in 1828 and the Defence Ministry in 1835. The Royal Palace (Slottet) came in 1848, even though Norway did not have its own monarchy. It was commissioned by the then Swedish king, Carl Johan.

Shaking off the Swedes

By the mid-1800s the very name of the capital became subject to Norway's ever-rising nationalism, with the 'Ch' in 'Christiania' gradually replaced by the more Norwegian 'K'. By 1880 almost all references were to 'Kristiania'. Then in 1925 the city took back its Viking name of 'Oslo'.

Before that, however, Norway had finally broken out of its union with Sweden, becoming a truly independent nation in 1905. The public voted to retain a monarchy, even though that meant importing royalty from abroad. Prince Carl of Denmark was chosen to be Norway's first modern king, and he stepped ashore in what was still Kristiania, with his British wife by his side and toddler son on his arm. To enormous celebrations they became King Haakon VII, Queen Maud and Crown Prince Olav.

World War I and the years just after it boosted the city's economy, given the demand for Norway's industrial products, but growth slowed again in the 1920s. The 1930s brought

Trams and tourism

As Oslo started to expand, development was aided by the introduction of an electric tram system. The tram linked the outlying areas, and gave easier access to the vast forest areas, called *marka*, which surrounded the city. The tram set off a hiking and skiing boom, and opened the area to tourism. Today's landmark Holmenkollen Park Hotel, near the ski jump, dates from 1894.

economic crisis, leading to violent labour conflicts. Even so, roads and parks were approved, along with some public housing and government buildings, many using the new architectural style known as 'functionalism'. Work on a new City Hall began in 1931.

Independence Lost Again

A gradual recovery from the Depression of the 1930s ended brutally with the German invasion on 9 April 1940. Oslo escaped extensive bombing during World War II, but thousands of German officers and troops were stationed in Oslo, and for five long years residents lived in a harshly controlled city. Oslo was kept dark at night, decked in Nazi propaganda, and food was strictly rationed, along with everything else. The Jewish population was decimated and it took years for Oslo to recover from its occupation.

A post-war baby boom created a sharp rise in demand for housing and in 1948 the city merged with neighbouring Aker. Large areas were set aside for more housing projects north of the city in Groruddalen and on the eastside at places like Lambertseter and Bøler. The economy started improving, Oslo's City Hall finally opened in 1950

A Modern Royal Romance

In 2000, Crown Prince Haakon announced that he had a girlfriend, Mette Marit Tjessem Høiby. The announcement caused something of a stir in royal circles, because Mette Marit came from anything but a royal background – she had been active in Oslo's 'house party' scene and was a single mother. Even so, the couple moved in together and married in August 2001, after the crown princess tearfully apologised for her wild past. The couple now have two more children, including the next heir to the throne after Haakon, Princess Ingrid Alexandra.

after years of delays, and in 1952 Oslo hosted the Winter Olympics, adding an updated Holmenkollen Ski Jump to the city's landscape along with new sports facilities and housing complexes.

The reconstruction led to the demise of many historic buildings in the 1950s and 60s, something city preservationists still regret. Oslo sprawled in all directions.

Free and Affluent at Last

The discovery of oil in the 1960s transformed Norway from one of Europe's poorest countries to one of its richest. Oslo in particular prospered. In the 1970s and

Crown Prince Haakon and Crown Princess Mette-Marit

80s city patriots clamoured for renewed attention to Oslo's historic central areas, setting off a wave of renovation that is still rolling over the city. Areas like Frogner and Majorstuen had remained fashionable, but old flats were upgraded, and by the 1990s, the investment fuelled by Norway's oil wealth was spilling over into suddenly trendy areas like Grünerløkka and Kampen.

Attention turned also to the waterfront, where the Aker Shipyard was reborn as the Aker Brygge complex. It gave birth to a major redevelopment plan for Oslo's entire waterfront, which is still in progress. The site of the earliest settlements at Bjørvika, behind the Akershus Fortress, is now part of the

Wearing the bunad, traditional folk dress

redevelopment. Oslo's Opera House is its cornerstone and a symbol of a city returning to where the earliest settlements first began.

A Terrorist Attack

The city's confidence was shaken badly on 22 July 2011 when a bomb exploded close to the office of Norway's prime minister, killing eight people and injuring more than 200. Less than two hours later, the bomber struck again, this time at a summer youth camp for the ruling Norwegian Labor Party on the island of Utøya where he gunned down 69 and left more than a hundred wounded, many of them seriously. Norway in general and Oslo in particular was plunged into a state of profound grief and shock.

The man responsible for the attack, a right-winger named Anders Breivik, admitted carrying out the killing as a challenge to Norway's policies relating to immigration and multiculturalism. He was convicted in August 2012 and sentenced to 21 years of preventative detention, with the possibility of five-year extensions to the sentence as long as he remained a threat to society.

The overwhelming reaction of ordinary Norwegians and political figures to the attack was a call for greater unity and tolerance, not less as demanded by Breivik. Although shaken, Oslo has for the most part returned to its normal, confident self.

Historical Landmarks

1500–500BC Early settlements emerge along the Oslo Fjord, leaving behind rock drawings known as *helleristninger*.

AD900 The first villages appear at the top of the inner Oslo Fjord.

1000 Official founding date for the city of Oslo.

1050 Viking king Harald Hardråde builds a royal compound near the mouth of the Alna River, at the northeastern tip of the Oslo Fjord.

1300 Håkon V Magnusson starts building Akershus Fortress and Castle.

1349–50 The plague ravages Oslo and the rest of Norway.

1380 Norway's last native king, Håkon VI, dies in Oslo.

1536 Norway becomes a province of Denmark, with Oslo as capital.

1591 Christian IV takes the throne in Denmark and becomes an active ruler over Oslo and the rest of Norway.

1624 Major fire destroys Oslo. Christian IV orders its rebuilding behind Akershus and renames Oslo after himself as 'Christiania'.

1735 The fjord at Bjørvika is filled in, to create land for new buildings.

1814 Denmark loses control over Norway, and a new Norwegian constitution is signed, but the country enters a new union with Sweden.

1866 The Parliament (Stortinget) is completed.

1877 First official use of the city's name spelled as 'Kristiania', using the more Norwegian 'K'.

1901 First Nobel Peace Prize awarded in Oslo.

1905 Norway breaks union with Sweden. Haakon VII arrives in Oslo.

1925 Oslo takes back its Viking name.

1940–5 Occupation during World War II.

1952 Oslo hosts the Winter Olympics.

1969 Oil discovered in Norwegian sector of the North Sea.

2000 Oslo celebrates its 1,000th anniversary.

2006 Ibsen Museum reopens, and the playwright is celebrated all year.

2008 The Opera House opens at Bjørvika as part of a major waterfront redevelopment.

2011 A terrorist attack on Oslo on 22 July by a right-wing extremist results in 77 deaths.

WHERE TO GO

Oslo is easy to get your arms around. Its city centre *(sentrum)* is compact, with most top attractions within walking distance. There is also a far-reaching and efficient public transport system featuring trams, trains, buses and ferries.

Most visitors stay in the centre, which is home to the majority of hotels. Oslo is a low-rise capital that sprawls over a large area, but its centre is firmly anchored by the main boulevard, Karl Johans Gate. This boulevard runs east from the central railway station (called 'Oslo S', for Sentralstasjon) up to the Parliament, the National Theatre and the Royal Palace. 'Oslo S' and the station under the National Theatre are key stops on the express train line that runs from Gardermoen airport north of the city. The stations are also starting points for excursions outside Oslo, although most suggested in this chapter (to the countryside of Hadeland, the mountains of Telemark, or south along the fjord, for example) are best taken by car or ferry.

THE CENTRE

A good starting point for exploring Oslo is the large open plaza called **Rådhusplassen** on the harbour side of the City Hall. The main E18 highway ran straight across it until the late 1980s, when traffic through the city was sunk into a multi-lane tunnel. Today the plaza is free of cars and open to the inner harbour, with its fishing boats, ferries and veteran ships.

City Hall
Oslo's majestic Akershus Fortress and Castle (see page 42) sit grandly above the inner harbour and arguably form the

Karl Johans Gate Street pedestrian

City Hall and Rådhusplassen

capital's most important landmark. The **City Hall** ❶ is Oslo's architectural heart and soul (Rådhuset; www.rft.oslo.kommune.no; open all year, Mon–Fri 9am–6pm, Sat–Sun 11am–4pm; charge May–Aug). The people working inside shape the city's landscape and guide its operations, and its soaring, mural-covered lobby is the city's premier venue for special events. This is where the Nobel Peace Prize is awarded (see page 12).

The City Hall dominates Oslo's inner-city skyline, its austere style attracting both praise and criticism. Detractors joke that it resembles two large blocks of brown Norwegian goat's cheese (*geitost*), but leading Norwegian artists of their time decorated the large complex inside and out. Artworks depict the country's history (statues of the Viking king Harald Hardråde on the western wall and St Hallvard, the city's patron saint, on the southern wall) and its cultural heritage (outdoor wood carvings adorning the walls around its main entry area). Much of the complex was built in the 1930s, and the labour movement is also glorified in the statues along its harbour side. The carillon in the eastern tower rings every 15 minutes, and on the hour plays a tune, often seasonally inspired music by Norwegian composers like Edvard Grieg.

The highlight of the City Hall, though, is seen immediately upon entering from its city side. The **lobby** is awash with light and colour, its ceilings and walls decorated by a long list of Norwegian artists. Much of their art depicts how Oslo moved from an era of class struggles and foreign occupation to post-war optimism and fellowship in building one of Scandinavia's leading social welfare states. Work began on the City Hall in 1931, but the building officially opened only in 1950, after delays caused by the Depression and war.

The circular street around the City Hall's main entrance on the city side is named **Fridtjof Nansens Plass**, after the polar explorer. The street leading into it is named after another Norwegian explorer, Roald Amundsen, and it is lined with shops, bars and restaurants, as well as the city's **tourist information office**. The first crossroads is found at one of two parallel streets that run through the prime central city area, **Stortingsgata**, named after the Parliament building and running parallel to Karl Johans Gate (see page 34).

Occupation frieze in the City Hall

The National Theatre, home of Norwegian drama

National Theatre

On the left after crossing Stortingsgata is the **National Theatre 2**, often called 'Ibsen's own' after Norwegian playwright Henrik Ibsen. The National Theatre opened in 1899 as the country's premier stage. It has been funded by the state since 1927, with its director and board appointed by the Ministry of Culture. The baroque-inspired building features the names of the three authors and playwrights over the entrance whose works were performed on opening night: Henrik Ibsen, Bjørnstjerne Bjørnson (who won the Nobel Prize for Literature in 1903) and Ludvig Holberg. Statues of Ibsen and Bjørnson stand on either side of the main entrance.

Inside, the theatre has three stages and a lounge in rococo style, with a large balcony facing towards the Parliament building further up a tree-lined mall in the city centre. It hosts the popular Ibsen Festival at the end of every summer, along with several productions of Ibsen plays throughout the year.

The plazas around the National Theatre also serve as a popular meeting place and a public transport hub in the centre of town. The airport train stops at the National Theatre station.

Across Stortingsgata from the National Theatre is the **Theatre Café** (Theatercaféen), a Viennese-style café dating from the time the theatre was built and adorned with drawings of Norway's cultural celebrities over the years (see page 109).

Stenersen Museum

Continuing up Stortingsgata, towards the park around the Royal Palace, will take you past several of Oslo's main cinemas. Just to the left down Munkedamsveien is the **Concert House** (Konserthuset), home of the internationally acclaimed Oslo Philharmonic Orchestra. Adjacent is the **Stenersen Museum ❸** (Stenersenmuseet; www.stenersen.museum.no; Tue, Wed & Fri 11am–4pm, Thur 11am–7pm, Sat–Sun 11am–5pm; charge). It houses art from a private collection that was donated to the city by businessman and author Rolf Stenersen, an admirer and financial adviser to the artist Edvard Munch (see page 63). In addition to Stenersen's Munch collection, the museum's display areas feature works by many other Norwegian artists; Amaldus Nielsen and Jakob Weidemann among them.

Ibsen's Homes

Directly behind the modernist Concert House and Stenersen Museum stands an ornate white building that dates from 1884, with an

Ibsen's An Enemy of the People was on the theatre's opening bill

arcade of modern shops beneath it. This is **Victoria Terrasse**, a remodelled commercial and office complex that originally featured residential flats where Henrik Ibsen lived upon returning to Norway in the late 1800s.

Ibsen wrote *Lille Eyolf* and *Byggmester Solness* here before moving a bit further up the hill to a newer apartment. Victoria Terrasse was later sold to the state, which started using it for offices. It served as Gestapo headquarters during World War II and was feared as a torture centre for Norwegian patriots. It was bombed twice during the war, in 1942 and 1944, and the portion closest to the newly renamed Henrik Ibsens Gate (formerly Drammensveien) was destroyed. It was replaced in 1963 by a modern office complex for the **Foreign Ministry**, which occupies the older portion as well. Just outside the ministry's main entrance is a plaza with a statue of King Haakon VII that gazes down to the harbour and the Akershus Fortress.

In the Footsteps of Ibsen

Playwright Henrik Ibsen, Norway's greatest literary hero, returned to Oslo in the 1890s after nearly 30 years of self-imposed exile, mostly in Germany and Italy. He viewed himself as a citizen of the world and had grown frustrated by Norwegian habits and local politics. Upon his return, he established a daily routine of walking from his flat on the main boulevard now named after him, to Oslo's Grand Hotel for lunch at the Grand Café. His route is now decorated with citations from his works, emblazoned on the pavement. Fans are still fond of following in his footsteps, past the park around the palace and down Karl Johans Gate to the hotel. Ibsen died on 23 May 1906. His lavish funeral was held at Trinity (Trefoldighets) Church, and his grave can be found in the nearby Vår Frelsers cemetery where many other prominent Norwegians are also buried.

Ibsen lived the last 10 years of his life nearby, in a flat at the corner of Arbins Gate and the former Drammensveien. The building now houses the **Ibsen Museum** ❹ (Ibsen Museet; www.ibsenmuseet. no; Mon–Wed & Fri–Sun, Thur 11am–6pm, guided tours of Ibsen's flat on the hour; charge).

The Royal Palace

Ibsen could gaze across the street from his flat to the **Royal Palace** ❺ (Det

Guards at the Royal Palace

Kongelige Slott; www.kongehuset.no; reserved guided tours end June–mid-Aug, in English at noon, 2pm and 2.20pm Mon–Thur & Sat and at 2pm, 2.20pm and 4pm Fri & Sun; tickets sold at post offices, Narvesen and 7-Eleven convenience stores or online at billettservice.no, some last-minute at entrance). The palace sits atop a hill with a view down Oslo's main parade street, Karl Johans Gate, towards the Parliament building.

The palace was built between 1825 and 1848, commissioned by the Swedish king Carl Johan, whose statue is just outside the front entrance. The palace was used by later generations of Swedish kings, including Oscar I and Oscar II, during the period of union between the two countries. King Haakon VII moved in upon his arrival in Norway in 1905; it remains the official residence of Norway's reigning monarch.

The palace has three wings, all built in Empire style. The weekly Council of State between the king and government is held here every Friday at 11am. The royal couple lives in a spacious apartment on the third and fourth floor to the left of the main entrance. The palace also features offices for staff members, a chapel where royal christenings and confirmations are held, and a ballroom and banquet hall which host state dinners and gala affairs such as the wedding of Crown Prince Haakon and Crown Princess Mette-Marit in 2001. The ballroom is included on the **tour** of the palace, along with the chambers used for the Council of State, the formal reception room known for its frescos of birds, the banquet hall and other public rooms. The **park** around the palace is open all year, and relatively informal changing of the guard ceremonies occur throughout the day.

Karl Johans Gate

The boulevard leading back into the city centre from the Royal Palace is **Karl Johans Gate**. It was named after the Swedish king, but altered to use the Norwegian 'K', rather than the Swedish 'C'. It runs through the core of the capital, beginning at the central railway station and leading up to

Constitution Day

Norway's Constitution Day on 17 May is the most important holiday of the year after Christmas, and is royally celebrated in Oslo. Activities begin early, with champagne breakfasts in homes and restaurants, and ceremonies at dozens of monuments around town. The highlight of the day is the mid-morning Children's Parade (*Barnetoget*), featuring brass bands and youngsters from every elementary school in town. The parade, known for its conscious lack of any military presence, winds up Karl Johans Gate to the Royal Palace, where the royal family stands on the palace balcony for hours to wave at the crowds. Norwegians traditionally dress up for the day, many in their regional costumes, known as the *bunad*. It is a colourful display of national pride that is not to be missed.

Karl Johans Gate

the palace. The stretch from the Parliament to the palace is the most fashionable, used for parades and decorated for special occasions.

From the palace, Karl Johans Gate leads back towards the National Theatre and the original buildings of the **University of Oslo**, on the left. These buildings now house the law school and some graduate programmes. The building in the middle, called the **Aula**, was used for the Nobel Peace Prize ceremony until the early 1990s, when City Hall became the venue. Murals by Edvard Munch adorn its walls, but it is only open to the public during concerts and seminars.

The National Gallery and Nearby Museums

Behind the university buildings are two of the many museums in central Oslo. The **National Gallery** ❻ (Nasjonalgalleriet; www.nasjonalmuseet.no; Fri–Wed 10am– 5pm, Thur until 7pm; charge) on Universitetsgata, contains the country's largest collection of older Norwegian and international art, showcasing Norway's most famous artists. Here are such national treasures as Harald Sohlberg's *Winter Night in Rondane* and other landscape masterpieces from the 1800s, along with works by international artists. Edvard Munch has a museum of his own in Oslo (see page 64), but the National Gallery does have a room devoted to Munch and several of his most famous works, including a version of *The Scream*.

Nearby on Frederiks Gate, the **University Museum of Cultural Heritage** (Historisk Museum; www.khm.uio.no; Tue–Sun, Sept–May 11am–4pm, May–Sept 10am–5pm; charge), opened in 1904, houses many of Norway's antiquities, including Viking treasures and exhibits showing life in Norway from its earliest settlements.

The Museum of Applied Art (Kunstindustrimuseet; www.nasjonalmuseet.no; Tue, Wed & Fri 11am–5pm, Thur 11am–7pm, Sat–Sun noon–4pm; charge) is a few blocks north of the National Gallery on St Olavs Gate and features Norwegian and international applied art, fashion and design from the 7th century to the present day. A highlight is its collection of royal clothing, including wedding gowns.

Parliament

Norway's **Parliament** ❼ (Stortinget; guided tours July–mid-Aug at 10am, 11.30am and 1pm, Sat only the rest of the year, closed Dec–Feb; free) dominates the eastern end of the mall that runs through the heart of town. Completed while Norway was still in a union with Sweden, it has been the seat of the National Assembly since 1866. The building's Swedish architect combined Norwegian and Italian styles of the time, with a central edifice and two main wings. The highlight of a **tour** is the elegant main assembly hall (Stortingssalen), where Members of Parliament have their

The central edifice of Norway's Parliament building

permanent places. Another spot well known to Norwegian TV viewers is the so-called 'wanderers' hall', where politicians meet journalists and each other to discuss the issues of the day.

The mall that runs from the Parliament to the National Theatre is a popular gathering place year round. The plaza directly below the main entrance into the Parliament's assembly hall is called **Eidsvolls Plass**, after the town north of Oslo where the constitution was signed in 1814. The plaza is popular with sun worshippers in the summer and demonstrators all year round. On 10 December every year, a torchlit parade in honour of the Nobel Peace Prize winner ends here in the evening, and the crowd waits for him or her to make an appearance on the balcony of the suite at the adjacent **Grand Hotel** (see page 135) where the prize-winner always stays. The winner traditionally waves to the crowd and accepts cheers and applause, before stepping

One of Vigeland's windows

back inside to attend the annual Nobel banquet at the hotel.

The Parliament is just down the street (Akersgata) from the complex that houses most of the executive branch of the **Norwegian government**, or Regjeringskvartalet (built 1958–1996). At the top of the tallest building is the office of the Prime Minister, and many of the key government ministries are scattered around it. Located between the Prime Minister's office, and just across the street from two of Norway's largest newspaper offices, are the Finance Ministry and the Supreme Court.

It is not unusual to see top government officials, including the Prime Minister, walking along Akersgata to or from Parliament. The entire area, though, also has a system of underground tunnels connecting the Parliament to administrative offices and those of politicians.

The Cathedral and the Old City

Karl Johans Gate turns into a pedestrianised street as it continues from the Parliament east to the central railway station. It is lined with shops, restaurants and offices along the way, with the **Oslo Cathedral** (Domkirken; 10am–4pm) soon rising on the left. The cathedral was originally called the Church of Our Saviour (Vår Frelsers Kirke), and was consecrated in 1697. An unknown Dutch master designed the cathedral's altarpiece and cylindrical pulpit, with the work carried out by Norwegian wood-carvers. The interior walls of the cathedral are white-washed, providing a contrast to the richly decorated ceilings and royal pew in baroque style. The stained-glass windows are the work of the artist Emanuel Vigeland, and were created in the early 1900s.

The bazaar halls around the back of the cathedral were built in the mid-1800s. The cathedral is the site of royal weddings and major state events, along with regular religious services on Sundays.

While the area to the south and east of the cathedral has a reputation for pickpockets, especially late at night, it is also the city's most historic and should not be overlooked. A short walk south along the street Kirkegata will bring you to the area behind the Akershus Fortress and Castle called **Kvadraturen**, a grid of streets with buildings dating back to the 1600s.

A courtyard in the Old City

The entire area was built under orders from the Danish King Christian IV, who had power over Norway at the time. Oslo, which the king renamed Christiania after himself, had suffered a string of fires, and Christian IV ordered the city moved behind the fortress, with buildings to be made of stone rather than wood.

Many early buildings still survive, including the **Old City Hall** (Gamle Raadhus) at the corner of Rådhusgata and Nedre Slottsgate, and the building at **Rådhusgata 19**, now housing the Café Celsius, just across the street. The latter dates from 1626 and was originally a military hospital. Gamle Raadhus, built in 1641, is also a restaurant.

Back on Kirkegata lies a newcomer to Oslo's museum scene that bills itself as having the world's largest collection of miniature bottles. The **Miniature Bottle Gallery** (Småflaskemuseet; www.minibottlegallery.com; Sat–Sun noon–4pm; charge) was founded by a local real-estate tycoon and descendant of the family that founded Norway's Ringnes Brewery. He started collecting tiny bottles, and around 50,000 of them are exhibited in the three-storey building.

Further down Rådhusgata is a stately old mansion called **Statholdergaarden**, which now houses an elegant restaurant on its second floor and a Danish-style *kro*, or café, in its cellar. The building dates from the 1640s.

Astrup Fearnley Museum of Modern Art

Another block east and to the right, on Dronningens Gate, lies Norway's **Film Museum** (Filmmuseet; Mon 10.30am–5pm, Tue–Fri 10.30am–9pm, Sat noon–5pm, Sun 1–9pm; free) and **Cinemateket**, which shows vintage films and arranges special festivals and performances. The museum also features a café and shop.

Crime crackdown

The increasing affluence of Oslo has come with a rise in the numbers of homeless people, prostitutes and beggars on the street. Oslo's crime rate is low compared to most cities, but it is wise to exercise the same level of caution as in other cities.

Norway's state-funded **National Museum of Contemporary Art** ❽ (Museet for Samtidskunst; www.nasjonal museet.no; Tue, Wed & Fri 11am–5pm, Thur 11am–7pm, Sat–Sun noon–5pm; charge) is just two blocks away on **Bankplassen**. It is housed in the original headquarters of the country's Central Bank (Norges Bank) and features both Norwegian and international contemporary art with changing special exhibitions. Also at Bankplassen lie what is billed as Oslo's oldest restaurant, **Engebret Café** (see page 106), and the **Architecture Museum** (Nasjonalmuseet – Arkitektur; www.nasjonalmuseet.no; Tue, Wed & Fri 11am–5pm, Thur 11am–7pm, Sat–Sun noon–5pm; charge).

Visitors should be aware that Kvadraturen has been the site of open street solicitation (prostitution is legal in Norway), as well as petty crime. Police and city officials have tried to control the trade and even closed streets to car traffic after 8pm. The area is being revitalised, but visitors should use caution.

Norway's Defence Ministry lies just behind the contemporary art museum. A cobblestone street to the left off Myntgata, past the stables for Oslo's mounted police, will lead the visitor right through the walls of Oslo's grandest structure of all, Akershus Fortress and Castle.

ALONG THE FJORD

It is no coincidence that the city's premier landmark was built on the fjord, which was Oslo's lifeline 1,000 years ago. Property along the fjord remains highly prized, and the entire waterfront is constantly being revitalised.

Akershus Fortress and Castle

It was the Viking king Håkon V Magnusson who decided that Oslo should have a fortress at the top of the fjord where the settlement was located. Work began at the end of the 13th century, and King Håkon V himself moved in, making the new **Akershus Fortress and Castle** ❾ (Akershus Festning og Slott; fortress area: all year 6am–9pm; free; changing of the guards at 1.30pm) the first permanent royal residence in Oslo. The castle was built inside the fortress walls, which in turn were perched on a spit of land extending into the Oslo Fjord. Today, Akershus is the pride of Oslo – local residents have previously voted it their most popular structure.

Boating boom

Norwegians have a long seafaring tradition, and you cannot help but notice the thousands of boats on the fjord. Locals joke that it is almost possible to walk from island to island by hopping from one boat to the next. Growing affluence from oil revenues led to a boom in the number of boats sold in Norway, especially in the Oslo metropolitan area.

The fortress grounds themselves are rich in history and perfect for leisurely walks. The top of the walls offer panoramic views over the city and fjord, especially to the west, and it is a popular place for picnic lunches and sunbathing in the summer. Concerts and outdoor theatre performances are held during summer months in the inner courtyard.

Inside the fortress and castle complex are several

Akershus Fortress and Castle illuminated at night

important museums, not least the castle itself, **Akershus Slott** (www.nasjonalefestningsverk.no; early May–late Aug Mon–Sat 10am–4pm, Sun noon–4pm, guided tours on Thur the rest of the year; charge). The medieval castle is believed to have opened formally in 1319, and was remodelled into a Renaissance castle in the early 1600s. Visitors can wander through its large rooms and ballrooms, often used today for state dinners. The castle also contains a chapel and the Royal Mausoleum, where Norwegian kings and queens are interred.

Just before the entrance to the castle, on the right, is the **Norwegian Resistance Museum** (Norges Hjemmefront-museum; www.forsvaretsmuseer.no/nor/Hjemmefrontmuseet; Sept–May Mon–Fri 10am–4pm, Sat–Sun 11am–4pm, until 5pm in the summer; charge). The museum chronicles Norway's five years of German occupation during World War II, and the heroic resistance efforts by patriots both inside and outside the country. The museum portrays daily life

The Opera House

under occupation and displays authentic documents, photographs, posters and equipment used by resistance forces. Just outside is the area where the Nazis executed captured resistance fighters.

Back down the cobblestone pathway leading to the castle and Resistance Museum, in the main courtyard of the fortress, is an **information centre** that often features changing historical exhibits. Past the **pond** (Karpedammen), where concerts are often held, is the entry area used for changing-of-the-guard ceremonies. Visitors can also stroll around the castle for sweeping views of the fjord and the eastern harbour area.

A drawbridge leads out of the fortress complex on its eastern side and over to the wide open plaza called **Festningsplassen**, used for large events such as the Pope's visit in 1989. It is ringed by buildings from the 1800s that now mostly house military offices, plus Norway's **Armed Forces Museum** (Forsvarsmuseet; May–Aug Mon–Fri 10am–5pm, Sept–Apr 11am–4pm, Sat–Sun 11am–5pm all year; free). The museum details Norwegian military history from Viking times, through the numerous Nordic wars under Danish rule, the years during the Swedish union and from independence in 1905.

Waterfront Redevelopment

The fjord area east of Akershus – **Bjørvika** – is the site of ongoing construction projects, as the waterfront becomes more user- and walker-friendly, especially since 2008 when

Oslo's **Opera House** ⑩ (*Operahuset*; see page 83) opened. The Munch Museum and the city's main library are also due to move to Bjørvika during the next decade.

Ferry Trips

It is already possible to wander and explore the fjord from the tip of the headland where Akershus sits. This is where the cruise-ferries between Oslo and Denmark arrive and depart, but just behind their terminal, at **Vippetangen**, is a smaller transit centre for the ferries that head out to **islands** in the Oslo Fjord.

The ferries are operated by the city's public transport system, so a day ticket for a bus or tram can be used onboard. One of the most popular, and closest, islands is called **Hovedøya**, which features the ruins of a cloister built by English monks in the 1100s. Other islands include **Gressholmen**, site of

Oslo Fjord

a popular café and Oslo's first airport, and a host of others dotted with tiny summer cottages that now command high prices. The ferries are packed on warm summer days, so be prepared for long queues. One ferry route makes a round trip in less than an hour, for a refreshing and inexpensive boat-ride on the fjord.

Inner Harbour

Back on land, visitors can walk past a wholesale fish market and the Harbour Authority's offices, beyond the cruise terminal and back to the heart of town. The views down the fjord are spectacular, partially blocked only when large cruise ships are in port. Soon you will come to the **inner harbour**, full of veteran ships used for charter tours and fjord cruises. If you're lucky, Oslo's 'Tall Ship', the **Christian Radich**, will be in port, and open for inspection or even available for a scheduled cruise.

The inner harbour is also the departure point for the sightseeing boats that ply the fjord and the ferry service to the Bygdøy peninsula (see page 48), which is home to several more of Oslo's museums. Ferries leave from Pier 3 opposite the City Hall every 20 minutes during the summer and run from April to October. Tickets can be bought onboard.

Nobel Peace Center

On the western side of the inner harbour, to the left of City Hall, is the **Nobel Peace Center** ⓫ (Nobels Fredssenter; www.nobelpeacecenter.org; 10am–6pm; charge). The Peace Center, which opened in Norway's centennial year of 2005, showcases not only the Nobel Peace Prize but also Norway's role in international peace brokering.

While all the other Nobel Prizes are awarded in Sweden, Alfred Nobel decreed in his will that he wanted the Norwegians to award the Peace Prize. And so they have, since

1901, with a committee appointed by the Norwegian Parliament sorting through the nominations and deciding on the winner. The Peace Center is a high-tech, hands-on museum of sorts with information on the prize, its winners over the years and changing exhibits dealing with war and peace.

To the left of the Peace Center is the transit terminal for the ferries that run to the Nesodden peninsula across the fjord. The ferries do not take cars, only people and bicycles, and thousands who live on Nesodden use them every day to get back and forth from work or school.

Nobel Peace Center

Ferries also leave from here for the western suburbs at Asker, and other points along the fjord, including the seaside town of Drøbak (see page 78).

Aker Brygge

Next to the commuter ferry terminal is the bustling **Aker Brygge** waterfront complex of shops, restaurants, bars, residences and offices. It was the first big waterfront renovation project in Oslo, and its success spurred the massive waterfront development projects that will continue in Oslo until 2020.

Just beyond Aker Brygge is the Tjuvholmen complex, where you'll find the revamped **Astrup Fearnley Museum of Modern Art** ⑫ (www.afmuseet.no; hours vary, check website; free), which moved here in September 2012. The privately owned museum houses an extensive and representative collection of Norwegian and international post-war art, as well as changing exhibitions of Norwegian and international contemporary artists like Yoko Ono. The contemporary steel-and-wood structure that houses the museum wonderfully evokes the city's seafaring history. It is worth coming here just to see the building, which is every bit as appealing as the artworks it contains.

A walking and cycling path runs along the fjord, past the Color Line cruise-ferry terminal (ships leave from here for Germany and Denmark) and the private boat harbour, to the Bygdøy peninsula and beyond.

THE BYGDØY PENINSULA

Just across the fjord, but connected to the mainland, is Oslo's Bygdøy peninsula, a mostly affluent and remarkably rural residential headland, which is also home to some important museums. Here you will find Norway's authentic Viking ships, the country's largest open-air cultural museum and the museums chronicling the journeys of Norway's most famous explorers as they headed for the North and South Poles and tropical destinations in between. As the long-time summer estate of the royals, Bygdøy is rich in history, and an important recreational area full of hiking and cycling trails and popular beaches.

Getting to Bygdøy is easy. The most popular way, especially if the weather is nice, is via the ferries that sail from Pier 3, opposite City Hall, from April to October. There is also a regular bus service from town, the red city bus No. 30.

The Viking Ships
No visit to Oslo is complete without seeing some of Norway's greatest national treasures: the 1,100-year-old vessels housed

in the **Viking Ship Museum** ⓭ (Vikingskipshuset; http://www.khm.uio.no; daily 9am–6pm, early May–Sept, 10am–4pm rest of year; charge). Here, within walking distance of Dronningen dock along Huk Aveny, are the world's best-preserved Viking ships. They were excavated from three royal burial mounds south of Oslo, and are believed to have been buried in the 9th century to carry their deceased owners to the next life. Of the three vessels found here, the *Oseberg* and *Gokstad* ships, with their exquisite lines, are in the best condition.

The museum was built especially to display the vessels and is a model of simplicity. It also houses many other unique objects found along with the ships, including combs, personal items, cooking utensils, tools and an intricately carved carriage, the only one to be found from the Viking Age. Plans emerged in 2006 to relocate the museum to the waterfront

One of the Viking ships on display

Norwegian Folk Museum

at Bjørvika, but controversy erupted, and any move is unlikely for a few years to come.

Norwegian Folk Museum

Just next door to the Viking ships is the mostly open-air **Norwegian Folk Museum** ⓮ (Norsk Folkemuseum; www.norskfolkemuseum. no; daily 10am–6pm mid-May–mid-Sept, Mon–Fri 11am–5pm & 10am–4pm Sat–Sun mid-Sept–mid-May; charge). You can easily spend most of the day here. The Folk Museum is especially worthwhile for those visitors who do not have time to travel around Norway's rural districts, as it displays the various cultural traditions around the country. Visitors can walk from one village to the next, seeing authentic timber homes, barns and other buildings dismantled from their original locations in outlying areas and brought to the museum. There is also a stave church, and hostesses in the various houses greet visitors wearing traditional regional costumes known as the *bunad*.

Activities abound, especially during the summer months, with folk dancing, craftsmanship displays, music and traditional baking. There is also a vast collection of folk art inside the main buildings near the museum entrance.

Norway's urban culture also receives attention at the Folk Museum, with an entire neighbourhood from old Oslo now on display, along with an apartment house featuring residential styles from the 1800s to the late 1900s. Cafés and restaurants serve traditional Norwegian fare.

Maritime Heritage

Visitors taking the ferry to Bygdøy can get off (second stop) at the tip of the peninsula (Bygdøynes), where three museums dealing with Norwegians' fascination with the sea are located.

Several veteran vessels, along with nautical equipment, are on display outside a distinctive A-framed building, easily seen from across the water. It houses the **Polar Ship _Fram_**, and is known as **Fram Museum ⓯** (Frammuseet; www.frammuseum.no; daily Mar–Apr 10am–4pm, May–mid-June 10am–5pm, June–Aug 9am–6pm, Sept 10am–5pm, Oct 10am–4pm, Nov–Feb 10am–3pm; charge). The _Fram_, built in 1892, is billed as the world's strongest wooden ship, and the one that has sailed the furthest north and the furthest south. It was used for three polar expeditions: first by Fridtjof Nansen, 1893–6, then by Otto Sverdrup, 1898–1902, and finally by Roald Amundsen, the first man to reach the South Pole, 1910–12. Visitors can go on board the vessel where displays tell the story of the expeditions.

Christmas in Oslo

The weeks leading up to Christmas are a magical time of the year in Oslo, and all over Norway. It is the darkest time of the year, which the Norwegians more than compensate for with open-flame torches, welcoming fireplaces, brightly lit decorations (almost always white, not coloured, lights) and widespread use of candles in homes, offices and shops. The Folk Museum's weekend Christmas markets attract huge crowds, as do special exhibits at Bogstad Manor and suburban Baerums Verk, a restored village west of town. Restaurants are packed with partying Norwegians enjoying the traditional _julebord_, or Christmas buffets, which feature special holiday foods. Outdoor ice-skating rinks often feature music, and there is often snow to lighten the landscape. The celebrations can go on into January.

Next to the *Fram* is a museum dedicated to another famous Norwegian explorer, Thor Heyerdahl. The **Kon-Tiki Museum**  (www.kon-tiki.no; hours vary; charge) is home to Heyerdahl's eponymous balsa raft. The explorer gained international fame for his daring *Kon-Tiki* expedition shortly after World War II, and the museum also features objects from his other expeditions, including the raft *Ra II* and statues from Easter Island. Exhibits relate his adventures and theories, and you can also watch the documentary Heyerdahl made about his 1947 Kon-Tiki expedition – the film received an Oscar for Best Documentary in 1951.

The Fram, used by Norway's great polar explorers

Heyerdahl, who died in 2002, was also an environmentalist who raised early concerns about the pollution of the world's seas.

Across from the Kon-Tiki Museum is the **Norwegian Maritime Museum** (Norsk Sjøfartsmuseum; www.marmuseum.no; daily mid-May–Aug 10am–5pm, Sept–mid-May Tue–Fri 10am–3pm, Sat–Sun until 4pm; charge). This waterfront complex tells the story of what remains one of the country's biggest industries, shipping, and how it developed from the seafaring Vikings to today's modern cruise ships and oil tankers. Along with the artwork, models and exhibits that let you go aboard, there's a worthwhile panoramic film that takes visitors along the coast of Norway.

The Holocaust Centre

A recent addition to Bygdøy's public institutions is the **Holocaust Centre** (HL-senteret; www.hlsenteret.no; daily 9.30am–4pm; charge) at Huk Aveny

56. This centre for studies of the Holocaust and religious minorities is housed in the historic Villa Grande. Initially built for industrialist Sam Eyde, the mansion later housed a ship-owning family. It was bought by Aker Township in 1921, along with the popular nearby beach called Huk, and purchased by the state in 1926. The mansion, with its distinctive tower that dominates Bygdøy's landscape, was supposed to house the state Meteorological Institute. The latter, however, preferred a site at the University of Oslo's Blindern campus. The building was taken over during World War II by Norway's infamous traitor Vidkun Quisling, who renamed it 'Gimle' and used it as his 'führer residence'. It later served as the French embassy until becoming a medical facility in 1948.

The building is now used as a research and communications centre tied to the University of Oslo, to focus on the Holocaust and other religious genocides, wars and violations of human rights. The centre features a permanent exhibit on the tragic fate of Norwegian Jews during World War II, and its capital stems from state funds paid as part of compensation for the wartime expropriation of Jewish property.

The Villa Grande houses the Holocaust Centre

Recreational Opportunities

Bygdøy is crowded in the summer, not just by visitors to the museums, but by locals enjoying its beaches and hiking trails. **Huk**, on the peninsula's southern tip, is one of the most popular beaches in the Oslo area, as are the slightly less crowded swimming areas at **Paradisbukta** on the western side of Bygdøy. Between the two is one of Oslo's major nudist beaches. Boat marinas surround much of the Bygdøy peninsula, and seaside trails are reached through the rural areas surrounding the royal summer residence called **Bygdøy Kongsgård**.

Another popular destination for walkers and cyclists is **Oscarshall**, built as a castle for Swedish King Oscar I in the mid-1800s, when Norway was still in a union with Sweden. Oscarshall, a pink, fairy-tale building that is floodlit at night, sits on Bygdøy's east-side overlooking the inlet of the fjord known as Frognerkilen. It remains at royal disposition, but sometimes opens to the public during the summer.

There are several places to eat and drink on Bygdøy. In addition to cafés inside the museums, there is a restaurant at Huk, another called Lille Herbern (www.lilleherbern.no; reachable only by a short ferry ride) near the Norwegian Seamen's Church, and the Rodeløkken café in an old wooden house on the water not far from Oscarshall. There are at least two eating options at the first ferry stop from City Hall: the Royal Norwegian Yacht Club and an outdoor café/restaurant at Dronningen called Lanternen.

FROGNER AND THE EMBASSY DISTRICT

The area behind the Royal Palace and across the fjord inlet from Bygdøy became fashionable immediately after the palace was completed in 1848. Called **Frogner**, it had been largely rural except for some small clusters of buildings used as villages of sorts for the sprawling farms of the time.

There were also summer villas in the area, used by wealthy people keen to escape the urban ills of old Christiania, as Oslo was called at the time. After the palace began being used, more villas were built, for use year-round. A remarkable collection of buildings arose along the streets now known as Parkveien, Inkognitogata and Oscars Gate, with several incorporated into what became known as **Homansbyen**. It is worth a stroll along **Oscars Gate**, from Colbjørnsens Gate to Bislett Stadium, to see the façades of apartment buildings and individual homes, which remain very fashionable (and pricey) today.

Many of them are now used as embassies or ambassadors' residences, like the mansion at the corner of Inkognitogata and Colbjørnsens Gate, which is the Swedish ambassador's home. There is heavy security along **Parkveien** as a result of the presence of the Israeli Embassy, directly behind the palace's park.

There is more security at the busy corner of Henrik Ibsens Gate (formerly Drammensveien) and Parkveien. The **US Embassy** was built here in 1959, designed by the Finnish-American architect Eero Saarinen (the embassy is due to move to a new, more secure location in Huseby and may indeed do so during the life of this book). On the opposite corner is the **Norwegian Nobel Institute**, where the Norwegian Nobel Committee meets to decide the winner of the Nobel Peace Prize. The building dates from 1867, and a bust of Alfred Nobel can be seen outside the front entrance.

Further up Henrik Ibsens Gate, at the busy intersection known as Solli Plass, is Norway's **National Library** ⓱ (Nasjonalbiblioteket; www.nb.no; Mon–Fri 9am–7pm, Sat 9am–2pm). The library contains material dating from the Middle Ages to the present day, and also hosts changing exhibits and cultural events throughout the year. The

Street-corner café in Frogner

building's decorative lobby
and main stairwell are covered with murals.

Oslo's 'Best West'

From Solli Plass, two main
streets extend to the north
and west. To the left is
Bygdøy Allé, best known
for its rows of chestnut trees
and fashionable shops. To
the right is **Frognerveien**,
which also winds by pricey homes, apartments, shops and restaurants. Together these streets are the main arteries through
Frogner, which is generally called Oslo's '*beste vestkant*', or the
best of the already attractive west side of the city.

A stroll up Bygdøy Allé from Solli Plass will eventually
bring you to a plateau of sorts, where the **Frogner Church**
stands rather regally on the left. Opened in 1907, it is one of
Oslo's largest, with more than 800 seats, and is often used as a
venue for concerts.

From here Bygdøy Allé slopes downwards, past numerous
embassies. Taking a right at the corner of Nobels Gate will
bring you by one of the grandest mansions in town at No. 28.
It covers an entire block and is the home of the US ambassador to Norway.

Vigeland Museum

Just behind the American ambassador's residence is a large
brick building with a wide lawn in front of it. This is the
Vigeland Museum ⑱ (Vigeland-Museet; www.vigeland.
museum.no; Tue–Sun, Sept–Apr noon–4pm, Tue–Sun May–
Aug 10am–5pm; charge), originally built as a studio and home
for the sculptor Gustav Vigeland (1869–1943).

Statue surplus

Gustav Vigeland was pro
lific, and one of the most
high-profile sculptors of
his time in Norway. He was
enormously productive,
so much so that a series of
statues meant to be placed
in the city centre grew too
large. They ended up in
Frogner Park instead.

The museum is devoted to Vigeland's works, and also hosts special, changing exhibits. The building where he had an apartment is open to the public, and there are displays showing how Frogner Park (and Vigeland Park within it) came to be.

The park lies just across the street from the museum, but its main entrance is around the corner on Kirkeveien: that is where the first-time visitor should enter, to get a feel for the magnitude of Vigeland's work.

Frogner Park and Vigeland Park

Frogner Park ⓳ (all year, 24 hours a day; free) was created in 1896, when the city bought the sprawling Frogner Farm from the Gade family. It was already well known in the city, not least as the site of lavish parties during its ownership by the Anker family in the late 1700s.

Vigeland Park

City officials planned to preserve the area as a public park, and in 1899 decided to add a sports centre as well. It retains a stadium for outdoor ice-skating, a swimming pool complex and tennis courts, in addition to open grassy areas, walking paths and buildings dating from the Anker family's time.

The 100th anniversary of Norway's constitution was celebrated in the park in 1914, and some statues started appearing, including one of former US president Abraham Lincoln. It was, however, the addition of **Vigeland Park** within Frogner Park that made it unique. Today it attracts more than a million visitors every year, most of whom come to see 212 of Vigeland's sculptures. Created in bronze, granite and cast iron, they seek to portray the essence and emotions of human life from the foetus to old age. At the centre of the collection is the impressive *Monolith*. Carved from a single block of granite and containing more than 120 figures, the 14m (46ft) high sculpture may represent the struggle for existence; others see it as a phallic symbol.

Vigeland himself also designed the outline of the park, and was meticulous in his details for the lighting, gates, pavement and fountains that accompanied his sculptures. Sadly, the park was incomplete when Vigeland died in 1943, but enough had been done to ensure that it is a faithful representation of his vision.

Oslo City Museum

Frogner Park also houses the **Oslo City Museum** ⑳ (Oslo Bymuseum; www.oslomuseum.no; mid-Jan–late Dec Tue–Sun 11am–4pm; free), which tells the history of Oslo from its Viking roots to the present. The museum occupies the former manor house where the owners of the Frogner Farm had lived. Special, changing exhibits and events are held in the ballroom, which was built by Bernt Anker at the turn of the 19th century.

A literary corner

A lot of 19th-century artists and writers lived in Majorstuen. Peter Christen Asbjørnsen (1812–85) of Norwegian fairy-tale fame lived at the corner of Bogstadveien and Rosenborggata. Amaldus Nielsen painted in his studio on Majorstuveien. Sigrid Undset, winner of the Nobel Prize for Literature, started her literary career in a flat at Vibes Gate 20.

The museum contains artwork, maps and dioramas showing how Oslo has developed since its official founding in AD1000. Interiors of Oslo homes through the centuries are on display, along with special exhibits on everything from King Olav's toys, to life in the city upon independence in 1905, to the history of the forests surrounding the city. Museum officials also arrange historically themed walks through various areas of Oslo throughout the year, and operate two off-site exhibits of preserved working-class homes on the city's east side.

MAJORSTUEN

Between Grünerløkka and Frogner, in the east–west arc called 'Ring 2', lie a few more urban residential areas with their own commercial cores: St Hanshaugen, Bislett (best-known for its stadium) and Majorstuen, to name a few. The **Majorstuen** district, to the northwest of the city centre, plays a central role in the city, because it has a major shopping street and public transport hub. It's best reached from the city either via the T-bane from the National Theatre or, for more of a view, the tram lines that run up Bogstadveien (try the No. 19). It is also an easy walk from the northeast side of the palace park, and that's the best way to experience the shopping area that starts on **Hegdehaugsveien** and becomes **Bogstadveien**. Most of Oslo's high-fashion stores are on this strip, and the Saturday crowds can be daunting. Better to explore on a weekday, if possible. The street is heavily trafficked, with cars and trams.

The area, roughly pronounced '*my-orsh-too-en*', developed rapidly in the mid to late 19th century. Originally it was outside the city limits of what was then called Christiania, and mostly rural, but a building boom that started in the mid-1870s led to new streets being laid out over the fields, with mostly three- and four-storey apartment buildings going up on both sides.

'Majorstuen' itself was a small wooden house on the site of what is now a major transport hub at the northern fringe of the district, on the busy street called Kirkeveien. The name stems from an engineer who had the military rank of 'major' and the Norwegian word for room or house, *stue*. The major's widow operated a café at the house they had built, which had the name 'Majorstuen' painted on the wall. The name soon applied to the whole area.

Majorstuen

Munch's The Scream

Bogstadveien cuts through the heart of Majorstuen. After crossing Kirkeveien, you will soon find the public transport museum, **Sporveismuseet** ㉑ (www.sporveismuseet.no; Sat–Mon noon–3pm; charge) on Gardeveien. The museum is housed in the old carriage halls for the tram and trolley system, and contains Norway's largest collection of vintage trams and buses from 1913. There are also some of the original horse-drawn trams from 1875, and visitors can go on board. It is a great place for railway buffs.

A few blocks away to the north is the headquarters of **Norwegian Broadcasting** (NRK; Tue–Fri 9am–4pm, Sat–Sun noon–5pm; charge), Norway's version of the BBC. Visitors can test their abilities as a weather presenter, news anchor or sports commentator, while guided tours take visitors behind the scenes to see how radio and television programmes are produced.

Just up the hill behind NRK is the **Blindern** campus of the **University of Oslo**. More than 30,000 students are enrolled here. The **university library**, called Georg Sverdrups Hus, is a relatively new addition, while the rest of the campus was built in the early 1960s.

Back at Majorstuen's public transport hub, where trains, trams and buses converge, the T-bane emerges from its tunnels through the city and starts heading up the hill to Holmenkollen. Holmenkollen is a major gateway for trekkers, cyclists and skiers keen to leave the city behind.

MULTICULTURAL NEIGHBOURHOODS

The capital's multicultural neighbourhoods have sprung up on its east side over the past few decades. Norway was a relatively homogeneous society until the first immigrants from Pakistan began arriving in the 1960s and 1970s. In 1992, there were 183,000 immigrants in the country, or around 4.3 percent of the population. By 2012 that number had grown to over 700,000, or 14.1 percent. Many of these arrived as refugees or guest workers, others as wives or husbands of Norwegians.

While the immigrant population is now fairly evenly spread around the city, many new arrivals from Pakistan, Turkey, Iraq and Vietnam initially settled east of the Aker River, in working-class neighbourhoods like Tøyen and Grønland. Today these areas, along with more inner-city districts, are known for their delicatessens, fruit and vegetable markets and the occasional mosque.

Munch's Works

The late Norwegian artist Edvard Munch is more popular than ever, a situation aided by the armed robbery at Oslo's Munch Museum in 2004. Oslo's Munch collection extends across a number of galleries, with particularly large collections on display at the National Gallery and the Munch Museum. A street copy of his famous *The Scream* adorns the wall of one of his childhood homes at Pilestredet 30B in the city centre, while original masterpieces can be found inside the City Hall, Stenersen Museum, University Aula and the Freia Chocolate Factory (Johan Throne Holsts Plass 1; open by appointment). While Munch's studio and last home at Ekely in Oslo's Skøyen district is not open to the public, visitors are welcome at his old summer home and studio in Åsgårdstrand, a 90-minute drive south of Oslo (Munchs Gate 25; Tue–Sun 11am–7pm in the summer, Sat–Sun only in May and Sept).

Tøyen and the Munch Museum

Tøyen, a short ride on the underground portion of the T-bane (metro) from the city centre, is perhaps best known as the site of Oslo's famed **Munch Museum** ㉒ (Munch-museet; www.munch.museum.no; Fri–Wed 10am–5pm, Thur 10am–7pm; charge). The museum, built to display the city's vast collection of paintings by the artist Edvard Munch, made international headlines in 2004 following an armed robbery and the theft of Munch's *The Scream* and *Madonna*. The paintings were recovered two years later.

Munch, who grew up on the city's east side and died in Oslo in 1944 at the age of 81, bequeathed all of his own art in his possession to the city. It was a huge gift, including 1,100 paintings, 3,000 drawings, 18,000 graphics and nearly 100 sketchbooks. The museum doesn't have space to exhibit it all at once, and plans are being laid to move the museum to new, larger quarters next to the Opera House at Bjørvika.

Next to the Munch Museum lies the **Museum of Natural History and Botanical Garden** (www.nhm.uio.no; entrance from Sars Gate; greenhouses and museum: Tue–Sun 11am–4pm, garden: Apr–Sept, Sun and hols 10am–9pm, Tue–Sat 7am–9pm, Oct–Mar Tue–Sat 7am–5pm, Sun 10am–5pm; charge for museum, free for botanical gardens). The garden and its greenhouses form an oasis in the middle of town, while the museum displays explain the evolution of plants, and there are dinosaur fossils, meteorites and precious stones as well. The museum also features animals common in Norway, and has changing exhibits.

Grünerløkka

The neighbourhoods of Rodeløkka, Grünerløkka and Grønland are all within walking distance of the museums at Tøyen, with **Grünerløkka** to the west arguably the most popular. This was originally a working-class district of Oslo that since the 1990s has become one of its trendiest neighbourhoods.

Some call it Oslo's version of New York's Greenwich Village. It is packed with cafés, bars, restaurants, galleries and shops of both Norwegian and foreign persuasion. The city's chief 'head shop' opened here years ago, and it has since been joined by a jumble of 'alternative' enterprises that occupy the street level of apartment buildings from the late 1800s.

The district's two main north–south arteries are **Thorvald Meyers Gate** and **Markveien**. Edvard Munch lived on the former with his family at No. 48 in the late 1870s and further down the street at Schous Plass 1 in the late 1880s. Markveien is perhaps the more stylish street, with fine dining spots, cool shops and lovely façades (check out those from Nos 16 to 22).

A block west of Markveien runs **Fossveien**, where Munch lived in his youth at Nos 7 and 9. The Aker River itself runs

A forest in Nordmarka

just west of Fossveien, clearing the way for views over to the **Gamle Aker Church** ㉓ (Akersbakken 26) – the city's oldest remaining church, dating from 1066 – and the riverfront park with foot and cycling paths that run all the way up to the hills of Nordmarka (see page 71). At the corner of Helgesens Gate begins the **Seildugsfabrik**, a brick commercial complex built in 1856, which once housed a factory producing ships' sails and has since been converted into a school. The building is a nice landmark to the neighbourhood's working class roots and a wonderful example of old industrial architecture, with a plaque outside that relates how in 1885 the factory's workers were paid a pittance.

A few blocks back east and north of the factory, at Thorvald Meyers Gate 15, is the **Norway Says shop**, a showcase for Norwegian design. Even when the shop's closed, it's worth strolling by its corner location to catch a glimpse of hot new artefacts and products from some of the world's greatest designers, who just happen to be Norwegian. Their work has been praised and promoted by Crown Princess Mette-Marit and *Wallpaper* magazine, among others.

Stylish homeware on display in the Norway Says shop

This upper portion of Thorvald Meyers Gate is full of other trendy shops and watering holes. The street runs by another park, **Birkelunden**, and down to the heart of Grünerløkka, **Olaf Ryes Plass**, a grassy square ringed by restaurants and cafés. Munch's mobile family lived at No. 4 from 1882 to 1883.

Several pedestrian bridges cross the river just northwest

of the Anker Bridge at the foot of Markveien. On the other side of the river on Hausmanns Gate is the **Norwegian Centre for Design and Architecture** ㉔ (Norsk Design og Arkitektursenter; www.doga. no; Mon, Tue & Fri 10am–5pm, Wed–Thur 10am–8pm, Sat–Sun noon–5pm; free). This is another showcase for Norwegian and international design and architecture, housed inside a refurbished electrical transformer station on the river. There is a popular restaurant and café here (Elvebredden, meaning the river bank) and another nearby (Mecca) in a green oasis with what could be Oslo's most idyllic outdoor café location.

Norwegian Centre for Design and Architecture in Grünerløkka

Grønland

Just southeast of Grünerløkka is **Grønland**, where east meets west in Oslo, in more ways than one. The area probably got its name from green fields, or land, along the Aker River – the traditional boundary between Oslo's east and west sides – which empties into the fjord on Grønland's western boundary. The area is no longer very green, having given way to asphalt and high-density living centuries ago. This is where many of Oslo's earlier immigrants settled.

Grønland

The area underwent a major refurbishment in the 1990s and is becoming rather fashionable, with housing developments springing up just behind the waterfront redevelopment area at Bjørvika. Oslo residents often head for Grønland to buy speciality foods, meats and, not least, fruit and vegetables from Middle Eastern and Asian vendors.

What was billed as 'Oslo's most exotic shopping centre', the **Grønland Bazaar**, opened here in 2006. In addition to Middle Eastern sweet shops and Bollywood.no – a shop selling Bollywood films and posters – shoppers can find a halal butcher, a vendor of Persian rugs, jewellery from Turkey and an Arabian restaurant. The bazaar, in the middle of the neighbourhood's main boulevard (also called Grønland), was built across a side street from the old police station, which now houses the **International Cultural Centre and Museum** (Tue–Fri 10am–4pm, Thur until 6pm, Sat–Sun noon–4pm; free). The museum has displays on Oslo's immigrant and multicultural history.

There are several other historic buildings of interest in Grønland, among them **Asylet** at Grønland 28, a two-storey half-timbered house built as a private merchant's home in 1740. It was later used as a courthouse, child welfare centre and hospital and is now a community hall and café. At No. 12B is an old apartment building from 1861, which is Oslo's oldest preserved workers' housing complex. It formerly contained 37 one-room flats; now all shops and offices. The Goethe Institute, a German cultural organisation, is located at No. 16.

Gamlebyen

On the eastern fringe of Grønland is another historic area, **Gamlebyen** ('the old city'). This is where ancient Oslo began, and ruins of its old churches and several buildings now make up the **Medieval Park ㉕** (Middelalderparken; outdoor areas open all year, guided tours late May–Sept, hours vary, generally Wed at 6pm and Sun at 1pm; charge), which runs along a lagoon near Sørenga and into the surrounding urban area. At the corner of Bispegata and Oslo Gate are more ruins plus the old bishop's residence and **Oslo Ladegård**, a manor house from 1725 built on a foundation from the 1200s that has also housed royalty. It is sometimes used for medieval-inspired concerts in the evenings. The No. 18 and 19 trams run through Gamlebyen and continue past **Ekeberg**, a spot that offers a spectacular view over the city and fjord (see page 16).

THE HILLS AROUND OSLO

With a fjord, hills and vast forests on all sides, Oslo's location is unusual among national capitals. Few capitals can offer the recreational and outdoor opportunities that Oslo can, where skiers, hikers, cyclists or paddlers can take off on trails, forest roads, the fjord or quiet lakes within 20 minutes of the city centre.

Hiking in Marka

The hills and forests are known as **marka**, and are divided into various regions. The most popular are **Nordmarka** (see page 71) to the north of the city centre, and **Østmarka** to the east. There is also **Krokskogen** to the west of Nordmarka, **Sørmarka** in the southeast, **Vestmarka** to the west of suburban Bærum and **Kjekstadmarka** in the southwest. Detailed trail maps are available in most bookshops and many sporting goods stores, as well as at the city-centre storefront location of the **Norwegian Mountain Trekking Association** (Den Norske Turistforening, DNT, Storgata 3). DNT can also guide hikers much further afield, to the mountains all over the country.

The local chapters of DNT maintain the hiking trails (look for the blue directional signs and blue markings along the way), in cooperation with local ski associations (*Skiforeningen* in Oslo), which mostly take care of the ski trails marked in red. Cycling routes are generally marked with natural wooden signs and black lettering.

All these signposts along thousands of kilometres of marked trails make Oslo's hills and forests incredibly user-friendly. Distances are noted in kilometres, and it is very reassuring to be out in quiet scenic areas yet on clearly marked routes that are used by thousands of others, even though you may not meet another soul for hours.

At weekends, however, the trails closest to the perimeter of the city tend to be heavily used, and you will meet plenty of others en-route. There is a local saying, '*ut på tur, aldri sur*', which translates as 'out on a tour, never sour' (it rhymes in Norwegian), and Oslo residents tend to take it seriously. A weekend hike or cross-country ski trip is deeply embedded in the Norwegian culture, especially on Sundays.

These trails are also made popular by the easily accessible entry points into the hills and forests. Several public transport lines run directly to trailheads, while others have large parking areas nearby for those coming by car. Many people are lucky enough to live so close to the forests that they can simply strap on their skis at their own door and set off.

The most widely used entry point to **Nordmarka** is the area between Holmenkollen and the old timber café and restaurant called Frognerseteren (see page 73), both easily accessible from Majorstuen on the Frognerseteren T-bane line No. 1. The trip is a scenic one, and both are destinations in their own right.

Holmenkollen

The **ski jump** at **Holmenkollen** ㉖, with its adjacent Ski Museum (www.skiforeningen.no; daily Jun–Aug 9am–8pm, Sep & May 10am–5pm, Oct–Apr 10am–4pm; charge), is an extremely popular day excursion. The views over Oslo and down the fjord are simply magnificent.

Church in the forest at Holmenkollen

The **Ski Museum** nestled under the jump has exhibits that tell the history of skiing in Norway, and there's equipment from Norwegian explorers' polar expeditions. Other displays explain Olympic history in Norway and the royal family's involvement with skiing. The late King Olav V was an avid skier, as is the current Queen Sonja; today's King Harald prefers sailing.

Holmenkollen has long been a highlight on the World Cup circuit. On the second Sunday in March, a Nordic skiing competition takes place for two weeks and culminates in ski jumping. Thousands of Norwegians make their way up to Holmenkollen during the annual Ski Festival, especially on Holmenkollen Sunday, to provide an enthusiastic audience for top athletes from all over the world.

Oslo Vinter Park

Not far from Holmenkollen is the **Oslo Vinter Park** ㉗ (www.oslovinterpark.no), with slalom ski and snowboard slopes usually open from early December to Easter, depending on snowfall. Lifts bring skiers to the tops of alpine slopes,

Stuer

While it is smart to carry your own Thermos or water bottle and a lunch pack in *marka*, there also are several strategically placed *stuer*, or timber lodges, that serve drinks and pastries and are accessible only by foot. Many are only open at weekends, but others, like Ullevålseter in Nordmarka, 5.5km (3 1/2 miles) north of the last station on the Sognsvann T-bane line, are open most days and also offer sandwiches and warm meals. Nordmarka's Kikutstua, 12.5km (8 miles) north of the last station on the Frognerseteren line, also offers overnight accommodation, but it is so popular that you have to make reservations months in advance. Kobberhaughytta, also in Nordmarka, offers accommodation as well.

Winter in Oslo's marka

a terrain park with moguls and jumps, and an international-standard half-pipe for snowboarders.

Then there's the roughly 2,600km (1,600 miles) of prepared cross-country ski trails throughout all of *marka*. It does not take long to leave the crowds behind, with the trails extending deep into the forests, some 50km (30 miles) as the crow flies to the north, for example. Many of the ski trails closest to the city are floodlit at night, as is the Tryvann Winter Park, until 10pm. The trails are maintained and prepared by the city and local ski association free of charge, although locals are encouraged to buy membership with the ski association. Visitors are considered guests.

Frognerseteren

One of the most congested ski-trail starting points is **Frognerseteren**, best known, though, for its timber lodge and views over the city. Frognerseteren, elevation 437m

(1,433ft) above sea level, was originally the mountain farm for the Frogner Farm in town, and its owner, Thomas Heftye, built a villa on the site in 1867. He also moved several smaller timber buildings from the main farm up to Frognerseteren. The city of Oslo bought the property in 1889. The timber lodge dates from 1891 and houses both a restaurant and café that is best known for its apple cake.

A recommended trek, on skis in winter or on foot in summer, runs from Frognerseteren to Sognsvann. From Frognerseteren follow the signs for **Skjennungstua**, another timber lodge known for its home-baked bread; it is around 3km (2 miles) further to **Ullevålseter**, yet another lodge, where lunch is usually available. From the lodge, it is 5.5km (3.5 miles) to the lake called **Sognsvann**, where you can catch another T-bane line back to town. The route is mostly downhill all the way.

Other Trails

Many local ski enthusiasts avoid Frognerseteren and Sognsvann because of the crowds. What they often do is take a local city bus, in winter and summer, to trailheads in **Sørkedalen** and **Maridalen** (from Hammeren and Skar, for example), or into **Østmarka** from a variety of points like Skullerud. The ski association offers a weekend one-way bus service during the winter to **Ringkollen** and **Mylla**, for long-distance skiers who ski their way back to the city (about 30–45km/20–30 miles). With such vast forests

Ski jump at Holmenkollen

at hand, lovers of the outdoors are limited only by
their imagination.

EXCURSIONS

Renting a car in Oslo can be
an expensive affair, but it can
also offer freedom to explore
some of the surrounding
countryside. Here are some
suggestions for a day trip
outside the city.

Frognerseteren

Hadeland

One of Norway's most visited tourist destinations is the
Hadeland Glassworks ❷ (Hadeland Glassverk, Jevnaker;
www.hadeland-glassverk.no; mid-Jun–mid-Aug Mon–Sat
10am–5pm, Sun 11am–6pm, shorter hours rest of year), where
glass-blowers have been creating everything from goblets to
works of art since 1762. The restored factory and adjacent
shops attract more than half a million visitors a year.

The glassworks is located in the town of **Jevnaker** on the
scenic **Randsfjord**, about an hour's drive (66km/41 miles)
northwest of Oslo. Getting there will take you through suburban Bærum and over the hills of Sollihøgda on the E16
highway. Just after Sollihøgda, on a clear day the drive offers
fine views over the **Tyrifjord** towards the mountains. Take
off at Sundvollen and follow signs for **Kleivstua** (up a short
toll road; have some 10-kroner coins handy) for an even more
spectacular view from the top of the western edge of the
Krokskogen forest.

Back down on the E16, continue towards Hønefoss, taking off at the sign for Jevnaker, Highway 241. This is another

scenic road though a rural area. Before arriving in Jevnaker, you may want to stop at the **Kistefos Museum** (Kistefos-Museet; www.kistefos.museum.no; late May–early Oct Tue–Sun 11am–5pm; charge), a former pulp factory that is now an industrial museum, art gallery and sculpture park.

Hadeland is the name of this scenic district, which also features medieval churches, like the **Sister Churches** at **Granavollen**, and its own outdoor folk museum, the **Hadeland Folkemuseum** (June–Aug Tue–Fri 11am–4pm, Sat–Sun noon–4pm; charge), at **Jaren**. The entire area offers sweeping views over a unique cultural landscape that some call 'Norway's Tuscany'. It is easy to follow Highway 4 back south to Oslo. For more information on Hadeland, go to visithr.no.

Blaafarvevaerket and Eggedal

Another excellent day trip from Oslo that could easily be extended into an overnight visit, is the drive west to Drammen and up Highways 283 and 35 to **Åmot** ㉙ (72km/45 miles) and its historic cobalt mine museum. Called **Blaafarvevaerket**, the 'Blue Colour Works', this 18th century industrial area is now the site of special art exhibitions every summer. The old factory area is open from late May to late September, daily from 11am (charge), as are adjacent historic areas and the old cobalt mine itself a few kilometres away.

The drive takes around an hour, and it is wise to arrive early, as it's a popular destination for locals all summer long. In addition to the main art exhibit, usually featuring prominent Scandinavian artists, there are shops and a café serving traditional Norwegian foods, a petting zoo for children and picnic areas along the river.

There is also a historical area and waterfall a short walk up the river. Tours are available through the old mine.

Hadeland, 'Norway's Tuscany'

The road past Blaafarvevaerket continues through the valley of **Sigdal** up to **Eggedal**, an area popular with artists. The former homes of artists Theodor Kittelsen and Christian Skredsvig, the latter in Eggedal, are open to the public during summer. There is also a folk museum in Sigdal, and you can get a taste of the Norwegian mountains just beyond Eggedal at **Tempelseter**, located on the western slope of the mountain known as **Norefjell**, which is popular with hikers and skiers.

Eidsvoll

In 1814, the founding fathers of modern Norway gathered at an estate in **Eidsvoll** ⓮, 74km (46 miles) north of Oslo, to hammer out the country's first constitution. It took another 91 years before Norway finally emerged as a fully independent country, but the signing of the constitution on 17 May 1814 was a pivotal event, and the estate is a national landmark.

The **Eidsvoll Building** (www.eidsvoll1814.no; May–Aug daily 10am–5pm, Sept–Apr Tue–Fri 10am–3pm, Sat–Sun noon–5pm, Oct–Mar closed Tue; charge) is about an hour's drive north of Oslo, just beyond the airport at Gardermoen, via the E6 highway. Tours are available, telling the history of the constitution and the men who were behind it. Visitors wander through the rooms of the manor house where the constitutional meetings took place. The grounds feature more exhibits, as well as a shop and café.

For an overnight excursion, continue on the E6 highway north along Norway's largest lake, Mjøsa, to Hamar and Lillehammer, which sprung to international attention during the 1994 Winter Olympics. The speed-skating events were held at **Hamar** in the 'Viking Ship' arena, which resembles an overturned Viking ship. Hamar also has a museum of Norwegian emigration and a folk museum. The town of **Lillehammer**, at the northernmost end of Lake Mjøsa, has an Olympic museum, an excellent city art museum and the Maihaugen open-air museum, along with its picturesque, pedestrianised main street.

Drøbak and Oscarsborg

You don't need a car to visit the seaside village of **Drøbak** ③, an hour south of Oslo on the eastern side of the Oslo Fjord. A ferry service, which also offers fine sightseeing along the fjord, runs in summer from the inner harbour in front of City Hall. Buses are also available, as many Drøbak residents commute to Oslo to work. Travelling by car offers the most flexibility, though, and makes it easier to visit inland areas as well.

Xmas every day

A highlight of Drøbak is its Julehus, a large gallery and shop devoted to Christmas all year long, with its own post office for posting letters to Santa, called *Nisse* in Norway.

A German battleship was sunk by the guns of Oscarsborg

Drøbak features an old church, historic white wooden buildings and a host of shops and restaurants. The village also has its own aquarium, **Drøbak Akvarium and Marine Biology Centre for the Oslo Fjord** (daily June–Aug 10am–7pm, Sept–May 10am–4pm; charge). The aquarium features species from the Oslo Fjord and a tank where children can touch starfish, crabs and other marine creatures. There is also a special display on lutefisk, the preserved cod dish loved by some and despised by others (see page 101).

The nearby **Follo Museum** (www.follomuseum.no; mid-May–mid-Sept Tue–Fri 11am–4pm, Sun noon–4pm; charge) is an open-air museum displaying the cultural history of the area, and includes several old homes that are open to the public.

The boat to Drøbak passes **Oscarsborg**, a historic fortress on an island off Drøbak, from which a German battleship was fired on and sunk during the invasion of Norway in April 1940. Today the fortress and historic buildings are open to the public, overnight accommodation is available in the former officers' quarters, and meals are served in the officers' dining room. The island has a guest harbour, swimming beaches and walking trails, with a ferry service available from Drøbak and Sætre on the other side of the fjord. For details, see www.fors varsbygg.no/festningene.

South to the Swedish Border

Thousands of Norwegians head south on the E6 highway every day, especially at weekends, to cross the border for cheaper shopping in Sweden. The Swedish coastal town of **Strömstad**, 138km (86 miles) south of Oslo, is packed at weekends. Strömstad is an attractive maritime destination in its own right in summer.

On the way to the border are some landmarks well worth a visit, including an ancient fortress at **Halden** and the old town

Admiring the view in Telemark

in **Fredrikstad**. Either place makes a fine destination for a day trip from Oslo. There is also the much closer coastal village of **Son**, which is a picturesque spot, especially in summer.

Further Afield

Visitors short of time but anxious to get a glimpse of Norway's mountains and western fjords can take the train from Oslo and back on a tour known as **'Norway in a Nutshell'** (see www.fjordtours.no or www.visitflam.com for details). The excursion generally involves taking the train to the heart of the mountains at **Myrdal**, with a connection to the famed **Flåm Railway ㉜** down to the **Sognefjord**. From there it's possible to stay at the historic Fretheim Hotel or continue by boat through the fjord to **Bergen ㉝**, or up the **Nærøyfjord** to **Gudvangen** and the hotel at **Stalheim**, known for its stunning views over mountains and fjord. From there you can also go on to Bergen by bus or train, or return to Oslo.

Telemark is another mountain area that is fairly close to Oslo and makes for an excellent overnight trip. At **Rjukan ㉞** and **Vemork** (about 180km/110 miles from Oslo), the Norwegian Resistance sabotaged German efforts to produce enough heavy water for their own atomic bomb. A gondola at Rjukan affords fine mountain views.

Nearby is one of Norway's most distinctive mountain peaks, **Gaustatoppen**, with a trail to the top for the hearty. A railway, built by NATO at the height of the Cold War, also runs up through the mountain to a point close to the summit. A few kilometres away is the historic Tuddal Hotel, a timber landmark overlooking a lake, with an excellent restaurant.

On the way back to Oslo, don't miss the Heddal Stave Church at **Heddal ㉟** (on the E134 highway) – it's Norway's largest stave church (a medieval wooden Christian church). The historic city of **Kongsberg** is also worth a visit, with its silver mines and Kongsberg Church, which dates from 1761.

WHAT TO DO

Oslo is one of the world's most expensive cities, so it helps to be mentally prepared to avoid continual price shock. The high prices result mostly from high taxes, but some protectionist government policies and the relatively small market play a role. It's fully possible, though, to enjoy a night on the town or even go shopping without breaking the bank.

ENTERTAINMENT

Music, Opera and Theatre

Music **festivals** abound from May to September. Some of them are famous, like the 'Norwegian Wood' outdoor rock concert, the 'Øya (Island) Festival' and the Oslo Chamber Music Festival. Tickets are often sold out in advance (see www.visitoslo.com for concert schedules, ticket information and other entertainment listings).

The **Oslo Philharmonic Orchestra** has gained international attention for the quality of its performances. Its home is the modernistic Oslo Concert House (Konserthuset; www.oslokonserthus.no or www.oslofilharmonien.no) in the city centre. Many audience members are subscribers, but individual tickets are often available, especially well in advance. The season generally runs from early autumn to spring. There is also a vast selection of other events at the Concert House all year long, from appearances by visiting symphony orchestras, to international pop music and opera stars.

When Oslo's **Opera House** opened in April 2008, it was billed as the biggest cultural event in Norway since the construction of Trondheim's Nidaros Cathedral in the Middle

Oslo's Opera House became an instant landmark

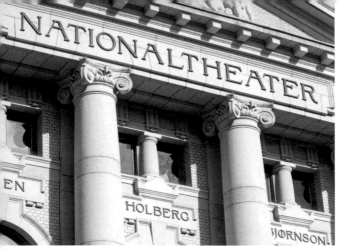

The National Theatre

Ages. The Opera, with its white marble exterior sloping into the fjord at Bjørvika, became an instant landmark, and visitors come as much to wander around and even on top of it (its roof is open to the public, offering views of the city and waterfront) as to hear its widely acclaimed acoustics inside. The Opera House also houses the Norwegian Ballet. See www.operaen.no for program and ticket information.

A visit to Oslo's **National Theatre** (see page 30) is highly recommended, especially during the annual Ibsen Festival at the end of the summer, when some plays are simultaneously translated into English via headsets. Even if you can't understand Norwegian, seeing a production of *Peer Gynt*, *Ghosts* or *Hedda Gabler* in Ibsen's native language can be a memorable experience.

There are quite a few small and charming theatres in Oslo, which feature ever-changing variety shows and comedy reviews, though only in Norwegian. **Chat Noir** (www.chat noir.no), not far from the National Theatre at Klingenberggata

5, is a classic old cabaret spot complete with cocktail service and little lamps on the tables.

Cinema

Norwegians are avid moviegoers, and seeing a film in Oslo is a civilised and stress-free experience. Tickets can be purchased up to three days in advance, seats are reserved, several cinemas have cafés that sell wine, and drinks can be taken into the cinema itself. Tickets for any cinema (*kino*) can be bought at any Oslo box office, as most are part of the Oslo Cinematographers' Association. Most open for ticket sales at 3pm, but the large, multi-screen Saga Kino in the city centre opens by 10am, just a few doors up the street from Chat Noir. All films are shown in their original language with Norwegian subtitles; there is no dubbing. Ticket prices vary, but are generally around NOK 100 for adults.

Just across the street from the Chat Noir theatre is the remodelled **Klingenberggata Kino**, which has one of Oslo's largest cinemas, along with several smaller screens in the complex.

Nightlife

Oslo is full of bars and clubs, with many staying open as late as 3am. The music scene blossomed in the 1990s, with Norway producing some of the world's most sought-after and imitated *elektronika* bands. Clubs like **Blå** (www.blaaoslo.no) on the Aker River near Grünerløkka (Brenneriveien 9C) are still going strong. They attracted international attention, and DJs flocked to the city.

Most of the nightclubs are concentrated in the centre, where they can stay open later than in the more outlying neighbourhoods. **Smuget** (Rosenkrantz Gate 22) is an institution, but the street where it is located can be a little seedy – take care. **Onkel Donald** (Universitets Gate 26) is popular, as is the nearby **Last Train** (www.lasttrain.no). For a quieter drink with lots of Arctic atmosphere, try **Fridtjof** (www.

fridtjof-pub.no), just across from City Hall at Fridtjof Nansen Plass 7. Even classier is lobby bar **Dagligstuen**, in the nearby Hotel Continental (Stortingsgt 24–26), where you can sip cocktails surrounded by Edvard Munch lithographs.

The trendy Grünerløkka/Grønland area has a lot to offer in addition to Blå, such as **Kaos** (www.cakekaos.no; Thorvald Meyers Gate 56), **Parkteatret Bar** (www.parkteatret.no; Olaf Ryes plass 11) and **Gloria Flames** (Grønland 18). **Südøst** (www.sydost.no) at Trondheimsveien 5 remains a hot spot in town for the beautiful people. **Fru Hagen** (www.fruhagen.no; Thorvald Meyers Gate 40) was one of the first cool cafés to open when Grünerløkka evolved from a working-class neighbourhood into a chic magnet for young artists and professionals. **Dattera til Hagen** (www.dattera.no) at Grønland 10 is always crowded, even in the early morning, and it has a popular dance floor. Nearby are the brilliantly restored pub and restaurant **Olympen** (www.olympen.no; Grønlandsleiret 15) and its adjacent nightclub **Pigalle**.

Over in the Majorstuen district, **Horgan's** (www.horgans.no) on lower Hegdehaugsveien (No. 24) often has queues out the door. There is a microbrewery a few blocks further up the street and to the left; **Oslo Mikrobryggeri** (www.omb.no) at Bogstadveien 6.

Many restaurants transform themselves into

Raucous revellers

A night on the town can be an eye-opening experience for visitors to Oslo. Given the sometimes prohibitive drinks prices, many prefer to buy in bulk and drink at home (known locally as 'foreplay'), before heading out to the bars. Many revellers are well-oiled even before the night has properly begun. Hard-partying Norwegians spill onto the streets after the bars close, and public drunkenness has been a problem for years. The street scene after midnight can turn violent, so police advise against any contact with late-night carousers.

Café culture

nightclubs late in the evening, and several impose age limits as high as 25. Cover charges are common, especially on weekends.

SHOPPING

Oslo is packed with trendy shops featuring branded clothes and goods, modern Scandinavian design and products, as well as traditional arts and crafts. Much of the latter puts a new twist on classic products like rose-painted bowls.

Norwegian Specialities

Sweaters, pewter, enamelware, linens, glassware and porcelain are Norway specialities and quality is generally high. The craft stores **Heimen Husflid** (www.heimen.net; Rosenkrantz Gate 8) and **Husfliden** (www.dennorskehusfliden.no; Stortorvet 9) deal in genuine handmade Norwegian items, not the cheaper imitations sold in many souvenir shops. Both also make

Paying the price

For several years in a row, Oslo has been ranked as the world's most expensive city by a variety of institutions, including Swiss Bank USB, the City Mayors' Association and others. The dubious honour is based on a 'shopping basket' of products and services. Oslo's food and drink prices are notoriously high, while hotel rates, curiously, can be lower than those in other major cities.

the traditional Norwegian folk costumes known as the *bunad*, of which many are on display. A *bunad* can take many months to make and be extremely expensive, depending on how elaborate its embroidery and silver jewellery are. It is an investment for life, though, and those with a *bunad* always know what they'll wear to weddings, confirmations, black-tie or dinner-jacket affairs and on Christmas Eve, not to mention 17 May (Constitution Day) celebrations.

The **Oslo Sweater Shops** (www.shopatnorway.com) at the Radisson SAS Scandinavia Hotel and the Clarion Royal Christiania Hotel, offer a vast array of machinemade sweaters, but most are made in Norway. **Oleana** (www.oleana.no) has a line of lighter-weight sweaters based on innovative designs, and sold at an Oleana shop at Stortingsgate 8, **Heimen Husflid** at Rosenkrantzgate 8 and at **Rein og Rose** in Vika at Ruseløkkveien 3. Moods of Norway (www.moodsofnorway.com; Hegdehaugsveien 34) is a much-celebrated Norwegian success story with its sideways glance at modern fashions and accessories.

Don't miss **Norway Designs** (norwaydesigns.no) in the heart of town at Stortingsgate 28. It is an institution, featuring Nordic-designed kitchen items, crystal, artworks, clothing and jewellery. The showplace is known for its elaborate displays at Christmas.

Norwegian jewellery is abundant, and several local stores are gallery-like places well worth a visit. Among them are the landmark **David-Andersen AS** (david-andersen.no) at Karl Johans Gate 20, **Thune** (www.thune.no) at Valkyriegt 13 with another outlet in Aker Brygge, and **Juhls Silver Gallery** (www.juhls.no) near the City Hall at Roald Amundsens Gate 6. Juhls specialises in jewellery from northern Norway, with its designs influenced by the Sami traditions of this region.

Shopping Districts

Bogstadveien, in the Majorstuen district behind the Royal Palace, is one of Oslo's most popular shopping streets, after the main drag **Karl Johans Gate**. Many of the traditional familyowned bakeries, stationery stores, fish shops and other necessary merchants have given way to trendy clothing stores, including several international retailers like Zara of Spain. The street remains packed with shoppers at all times, especially on Saturdays. **Skovveien**, which runs behind the palace, features many upmarket speciality shops, while **Frognerveien**, a bit further west, is also full of stores and crowds.

Flea market

The **Grünerløkka** district has become a mecca for shoppers (see page 64). Don't miss **Norway Says** (Thorvald Meyers Gate 15) for some of the best Scandinavian design of the past few decades. Rows of trendy shops are found along Thorvald Meyers Gate and Markveien, which run parallel to each other. **Grønland** is the place to go for more ethnic items, especially goods from Pakistan and the Middle East.

From the ethnic to the exclusive, **Aker Brygge** should not be ignored. This waterfront complex on Oslo's inner harbour is packed with shops and restaurants.

Markets

Apart from the established stores and shopping centres, Oslo also has various open-air markets. One of the biggest is at **Vestkanttorget** in the Majorstuen district. Stallholders sell sausages, antiques, artworks and handicrafts on Saturdays 10am–5pm. **Youngstorget** in the centre has market stalls every day, while there is a flower market at nearby **Stortorget**.

Christmas markets

There are several Christmas markets in Oslo every year, the most popular being those at the Norwegian Folk Museum on the Bygdøy Peninsula and at Bogstad Gård, a historic manor house in the valley of Sørkedalen, northwest of town but within the city limits. They are usually held on the first two weekends of December. Others are usually advertised in local newspapers under *julemarked*.

SPORTS AND ACTIVITIES

Many Norwegians are sports fanatics. Where else in the world will fans regularly camp out in the snow to get a good viewing spot at a cross-country ski race? Winter sports traditionally reign supreme, but most Norwegians are also mad about more summery sports like soccer, sailing and cycling.

Cross-country skiing in Nordmarka

Winter Sports

Skiing. This is the greatest local passion of them all, with miles of prepared trails in the hills above Oslo (see page 69). The Oslo Vinter Park has a variety of lifts, and offers slalom runs, special hills and features for snowboarders, and a terrain park with moguls and jumps. For more information contact the local Ski Association (tel: 22 92 32 00; www.skiforeningen.no).

Ice-skating. Outdoor ice-skating is available at several rinks around town in winter. Two of the most popular are the Narvisen rink, located between the National Theatre and Parliament in the heart of the city, and the much larger rink at Frogner Stadium, a short walk from the Majorstuen tram station. Skates can be rented, or even bought fairly cheaply at local sporting goods stores.

Sleigh rides. You can take sleigh rides over the meadows and through the woods on the fringe of town. They are usually group affairs and not available to individuals. Some sleigh

On a pick-up bicycle

rides (called *kanefart*, roughly pronounced '*kah-nuh-fahrt*', in Norwegian) run from Sognsvann up to Ullevålseter, or from Maridalen, depending on snow conditions. The Oslo tourist information office may have details, or check the 'What's On' section of www.visitoslo.com.

Summer Activities

Hiking. Oslo is a walker-friendly city, both in the centre, along the waterfront, and not least in the hills and forests around town (see page 69). Walking trails are marked with blue directional signs.

Cycling. This is a great way to get around. There is a rental system called the City Cycle Scheme. By paying a modest subscription, cyclists can pick up bikes at stands across town, borrowing them for three hours at a time. Special electronic cards can be obtained at tourist offices (see also page 116).

You can rent mountain bikes for longer treks in the quiet trails and dirt roads of the hills and forests around Oslo. Free cycling maps of Oslo are also available at tourist information centres.

Golf. There are several golf courses around town. Most are private, like the venerable **Bogstad Golf Club** (www.oslogk. no), but can offer reciprocal privileges if you are a member of a club at home. It may also be possible to arrange tee time at **Losby Gods**, a hotel and golf complex northeast of Oslo, with a scenic course set amid the hills and forests of Østmarka (www.losbygods.no). Losby, half an hour's drive from Oslo in the direction of Lillestrøm, is also an excellent starting point for hikes, including one to a local lake with fine swimming and canoeing opportunities.

Swimming

Public swimming pools are scattered around town, with the most popular outdoor complex adjacent to Frogner Park; **Frognerbadet** (Middelthuns Gate 28; late May–Aug from early in the morning; tel: 23 27 54 50; charge). The complex is best known for its high dives, waterslide and wide grassy areas for sunbathing. There's another popular pool complex near the Munch Museum and Botanical Gardens called **Tøyenbadet** (Helgesens Gate 90; open all year; tel: 23 30 44 70; charge), which has indoor pools, a sauna and exercise equipment among other offerings.

It is also possible to brave the clear but often chilly waters of the Oslo Fjord from beaches on Bygdøy and the islands reachable by ferry from Vippetangen. Water temperatures can reach 25°C (77°F) during a warm summer, but are normally lower.

Oslo's River Walk

The Aker River (Akerselva), which runs from the hills of Nordmarka to the harbour at Bjørvika, traditionally marks the divide between Oslo's east and west sides. The river played a key role in the city's industrial development and was where water-powered factories sprang up centuries ago. While most have long since closed, many have been converted to other uses, such as homes, offices, restaurants and clubs. A major effort began several decades ago to clean up the area, and today it is possible to stroll along a marked path from the top of the river, just below the large lake called Maridalsvannet, all the way to the harbour. Take the No. 12 tram to Kjelsås, follow signs to the 8km (5 mile) path and plan to spend an afternoon meandering back to the city centre, past swimming and picnic areas, office parks created from the factories, residential developments, historic bridges, statues and other landmarks. There are plenty of places to stop, eat or drink along the way. Guides to the area are available at visitor information centres and in local bookshops.

CHILDREN'S ACTIVITIES

Oslo offers a museum of art by and for children: the **International Museum of Children's Art** (Det Internasjonale Barnekunstmuseet; www.barnekunst.no; Lille Frøens Vei 4; Sept–Dec and Jan–June Tue–Thur 9.30am–2pm, Sun 11am–4pm, June–Aug Tue–Thur 11am–4pm, Sun 11am–4pm, closed Aug–Sept; charge). The collection has works of art by children from at least 180 countries. Children visiting the museum can also try their hand at drawing, dance and pottery.

Many other museums also cater to children, including the **Norwegian Folk Museum** (see page 50) and the **Ski Museum** at **Holmenkollen** (see page 72). The area around the ski jump has simulators that allow children and adults to get a feel for what it is like to zoom down a slalom slope.

The manor house and farm **Bogstad Gård** (www.bogstad.no; Sørkedalsveien 826; May–Sept Tue–Sun 1pm & 2pm; charge) has a petting zoo in the summer, along with special events in line with the season. The **Norwegian Museum of Technology** (Norsk Teknisk Museum; www.tekniskmuseum.no; Kjelsåsveien 143; Tue–Fri 9am–4pm, Sat–Sun 11am–6pm, daily 20 June–20 Aug 10am–8pm; charge) is a hands-on technological museum aimed at children. Most of the activities it offers are in Norwegian.

A youngster playing in Vigeland Park

Other attractions popular with children include boat-rides on the fjord and the **TusenFryd** amusement park (www.tusenfryd.no; open in the summer), south of town.

Calendar of Events

There is a lot going on in Oslo all year. For a rundown of specific dates, check the visitor information bureau's website: www.visitoslo.com. There are listings in English, and more information is available over the phone, tel: 23 10 62 00.

February. Holmenkollen Ski Marathon, a long-distance trek over the hills and through the woods from Hakadal, northeast of Oslo, to the arena at the Holmenkollen Ski Jump.

March. Children's Holmenkollen Day, a colourful and lively ski event for Norway's youngest skiers, some of whom can barely walk. Holmenkollen Ski Festival, a week of World Cup Nordic competition highlighted by ski jumping on the second Sunday of the month.

May. Constitution Day celebrations all over Norway on 17 May. In Oslo, the parade heads up Karl Johans Gate to the Royal Palace, where the king and his family wave at the crowds from the balcony (see page 34). The Abel Prize in mathematics, named after Norwegian mathematician Niels Henrik Abel, is awarded in Oslo later in the month.

June. Færder Sailing Regatta from Oslo to Horten; Bislett Games, international track and field competition at Bislett Stadium; Norwegian Wood Rock Festival at Frogner Park; Gay Pride parade.

July. Norway Cup at Ekeberg, the world's largest international football (soccer) tournament for children and youth.

July–August. Øya Festival, a major outdoor rock and club music festival, held in the Medieval Park (Middelalderparken); Ibsen Festival at the National Theatre.

August. Oslo Chamber Music Festival; Oslo Jazz Festival.

September. Major annual art exhibitions at The Artists' House (Kunstnerneshus) and the Oslo City Hall (Norske Bilder, Norwegian Pictures).

October. Nobel Peace Prize winner announced; Oslo Horse Show; Oslo Opera Festival.

November. Oslo Festival of Light; Oslo World Music Festival.

December. Nobel Peace Prize awarded on 10 December, the anniversary of Alfred Nobel's death, at the Oslo City Hall.

EATING OUT

Oslo's selection of cafés, bars and restaurants is remarkable, given the city's relatively small population. A restaurant and café culture has blossomed in the last 20 years and going out to eat and drink is now a primary means of socialising. As a result, most places are fairly full all week long and it's a good idea to book tables for dinner *(middag)*.

Oslo has just about every type of international cuisine going, from sushi and dim sum to tapas and enchiladas. The growing immigrant population has led to an array of Indian, Pakistani, Asian and Middle Eastern restaurants. However, when in Norway, try to sample local dishes made with locally grown ingredients, of which there are many.

Restaurants

The most important thing to brace yourself for when heading out to eat in Oslo are the prices on the menu. Even a relatively inexpensive restaurant is likely to set you back at least NOK 300 per person, more if you order wine. Dinner for two in most of Oslo's moderate to high-priced establishments will generally cost around NOK 1,500, up to NOK 3,000 at top restaurants for a three-course meal with an aperitif, wine and maybe a cognac with after-dinner coffee.

Why is everything so expensive? Most of it relates to Norway's notoriously high taxes. There's a 25 percent vat on every level of trade in Norway, and the taxes charged on anything considered a 'luxury' are very high. The taxes on alcoholic drinks are part of a long-standing government policy to try to discourage drinking. Food prices are also high in Norway, because it's a small market with protectionist policies aimed at keeping out cheaper foreign meat, poultry and vegetables.

Eating out on Bankplassen

However, going out to eat in Oslo can be a real joy, with a high level of service and food quality that takes at least some of the sting out of the bill. Guests are rarely rushed, as most restaurants assume that anyone booking a table at 7pm will probably occupy it for the rest of the evening. There is none of the 'feed 'em and move 'em out' mentality. That partly explains the high menu prices, since Norwegian restaurants don't have anywhere near the same rate of table turnover found in many other countries. Waiters will also usually wait until everyone at the table has finished eating before clearing away any plates, so that no slow eaters will feel pressured.

Many restaurants now have set menus, where you choose three, five or seven courses (sometimes even more), and most have a wine menu to go along with each course. Average menu prices are NOK 495 for three courses, NOK 695 for five courses and so on. Prices at ethnic restaurants tend to be more reasonable.

When to Eat

Visitors will almost always be served breakfast (*frokost*) at their hotels, where a breakfast buffet is usually included in the room rate. Don't be surprised by the amount of fish on offer: Norwegians often enjoy different types of herring, anchovies and smoked salmon with their morning meal. Most hotels will offer a variety of breads, cheeses, tomatoes, cucumber and boiled eggs, along with milk, coffee, tea and juice. The idea is to make your own open-face sandwiches, with a minimum of fried foods. More elaborate breakfast buffets may also offer fried or scrambled eggs, bacon and ham, pastries and fruit.

Cafés are locally owned and run

Lunch (*lunsj*) has never been a big deal in Norway, but it's catching on, and more restaurants and cafés have started opening up in the middle of the day. Lunch is usually served from 11.30am, with open-face sandwiches as a main item on offer, alongside a range of cheaper, light meals. The mainstays are shrimps piled up on white bread with mayonnaise and dill; smoked salmon served over cold scrambled eggs on bread; and roast beef on dark bread with capers and beetroot. There are also takeaway joints all over town offering everything from kebabs to burgers.

The main meal of the day is dinner. Most restaurants open at 5 or 6pm, although some open earlier and offer a cheaper set menu from 4 to 6pm.

Seasonal Specialities

The food in local markets and restarants tends to be heavily influenced by Norway's seasons. Autumn and winter are the time for meat and wild game, thick stews and roasts with all the trimmings. Spring and summer usher in lighter fare, with meals often served cold, like the popular local shellfish platters or simply cold cooked shrimps that diners peel and place on white bread with butter, mayonnaise and freshly squeezed lemon juice.

Seafood

Seafood is plentiful and of high quality, no matter what time of year. Norway is famous for its salmon (*laks*) and cod (*torsk*), but there are many other types of fresh fish and shellfish available. Some say the *breiflabb* (angler) tastes like lobster, while *steinbit* (monkfish) is another, less expensive white fish that is served in an endless number of ways. *Sei* (pollack) is widely available and cheap by Norwegian standards, even though it has gained panache as a favoured ingredient of top local chefs.

A seafood bill of fare

Mackerel (*makrell*) is bountiful during the summer months, and a favourite in southern Norway, fried or grilled with boiled potatoes, a sour-cream sauce (*rømme-saus*) and the ubiquitous cucumber salad (*agurksalat*)

Shrimps and other seafood at a market

served on the side. Most grocery stores have fresh fish counters, and many fish stores still exist around Oslo, often offering warm fish cakes *(fiskekaker)* as a walk-away snack.

Fish soup is another Norwegian speciality all year round, usually served like a chowder; cream-based and with lots of fresh vegetables along with the chunks of fresh fish.

The Fruits of Hunting Season

Hunting is popular among both men and women. Wild game is a treat in the autumn, when reindeer *(reinsdyr)*, moose *(elg)*, pheasant *(fasan)*, venison *(hjort* or *rådyr)* and grouse *(rype)* are often on the menu. Game is often served with a cream sauce, boiled potatoes, sturdy green vegetables like brussels sprouts *(rosenkål)* and *tyttebærsaus*, a wild red-berry compote also called *lingonberries*.

Almost all restaurants will offer Norwegian lamb *(lam)* during the autumn when it is fresh, but it is a popular main course all year long. Norwegian lamb is tender and tasty. Purists in Norway often prefer boiling their lamb and serving it as *frikasée* with leeks, carrots and celery root, or as the popular *får i kål*, literally 'lamb in cabbage', simmered for hours with just some salt and pepper. *Får i kål* has been voted the 'Norwegian national dish' in public opinion polls, and is a Sunday dinner mainstay during autumn.

Pork is by far the cheapest and most widely produced meat in Norway, while fresh chicken has only been mass-produced since the early 1990s. It has quickly emerged as a popular main course in homes and restaurants.

Traditional Fare

The most typical Norwegian cuisine is connected with the Christmas holidays, but its popularity makes it available in local restaurants from as early as October. Many of these dishes stem from the days before refrigeration was widely available, and when people had to preserve their food and make it last through a long, hard winter. These dishes are now wildly popular, if only on special occasions.

The most famous (or infamous) dish is *lutefisk*, which is codfish that's been soaked in caustic soda before being rinsed, salted, rinsed again and usually then baked in the oven under close supervision to keep it from disintegrating. Perfectly made *lutefisk* has a firm but gelatine-like consistency, with the layers of fish gently breaking away from each other. Norwegians serve *lutefisk* with rock salt, chopped slab bacon and hot liquid

Jarlsberg cheese

Norway has become well known for its Jarlsberg cheese, which was first produced in Jarlsberg county, around 80km south of Oslo, in the mid-19th century. It is now exported worldwide and even made locally on licence in the United States to meet demand.

Norwegian salmon is a local speciality

bacon grease, mashed green peas called *ertestuing* and boiled potatoes. Aficionados like to have some *flatbrød* (flatbread) on the side, along with some mustard, a mustard sauce, brown goat's cheese or even molasses. Most people drink beer with *lutefisk*, accompanied by a shot or two of *akevitt*, the Norwegian firewater.

Lutefisk season usually runs from October to December, as does the season for *pinnekjøtt*, dried lamb ribs that are soaked and steamed and served with boiled potatoes and mashed *kålrabistuing*, a yellow root vegetable. *Pinnekjøtt* can be very salty, hence the ever-present beer and akevitt on the side.

Pinnekjøtt tends to be most popular among Norwegians from the west coast, and is the traditional dinner on Christmas Eve. Thousands of Oslo residents and Norwegians in the eastern part of the country, however, prefer *ribbe*, thick pork ribs prepared with the rind still on and grilled to a crisp. The ribs are served with boiled potatoes, sauerkraut (*surkål*) and steamed prunes and pears, again with beer and akevitt for the traditional '*skål*'.

One of the most unusual meals served around Christmas, mostly in western Norway, is *smalahove*. This is for the adventurous, as half a sheep's head will be placed in front of you, eye and all. Some love it, others detest it, most say the ever-present *akevitt* helps build up the courage to eat it.

Finally, try not to leave Norway before tasting *rømmegrøt*, a sour-cream porridge served with melted butter, cinnamon and sugar, often with dried sausages, flatbread and fruit drinks *(saft)* on the side. This ultra-rich dish was traditionally made for women after they'd given birth, and midwives would bring it to the women in a traditional wooden carrying box called a *tine*. That's now the name of the state dairy producer.

Drinks

There has been a growing tendency among Norwegians to move away from hard liquor in favour of wine, but strong locally produced brews continue to have their place as *brennevin*, literally 'fire wine'. Most famous, and potent, is the *akevitt*, a schnapps-type drink made from potatoes with a strong taste of caraway and high alcohol content. It is usually served with cold beer as a chaser, and caution is advised.

Akevitt is widely produced in Denmark and Sweden as well. You can tell a Norwegian *akevitt* because it is most often amber in colour due to its fermentation

Thanks for the food

'*Takk for maten*', which is roughly pronounced '*tock for mah-ten*', is an essential phrase to use if you're either a guest in a Norwegian home or the guest of Norwegians who pick up the bill at a restaurant. It literally means 'Thanks for the food', and should always be said to your hosts at the end of a meal.

in oak barrels. Some of it, the so-called *linje akevitt*, is even stowed on Norwegian ships that sail to Australia and back, so the *akevitt* can gently roll in the barrels for weeks on end. The name of the ship, and the dates that it crossed the Equator (considered a critical threshold for akevitt quality, are printed on the back of the bottle's label.

Norway also produces several liqueurs, the majority of them made from berries or herbs. One is called St Hallvard, a herb-based liqueur named after the patron saint of Oslo. Another local speciality is an aperitif called Frost that's made from the junipertype berries known as *krekling*. It can be taken straight or mixed with tonic water, rather like a non-bitter Campari.

Beer is available for sale in local grocery stores, but can't be sold on Sundays or late in the evening; the cases of beer are literally covered up if the store is still open. Purchase of all wine and spirits requires a trip to the state-run liquor stores known as Vinmonopolet ('The Wine Monopoly'). It's all part of Norway's anti-alcohol politics, which strive to make wine and liquor expensive and difficult to get. The

The Art of the Norwegian Skål

Norwegians don't casually say the equivalent of 'cheers' or 'bottoms up' and just carry on. Rather, Norwegians take their toasting seriously, and they'll be pleased and impressed if you know the ritual and follow along. First, raise your glass and look the person with whom you're toasting straight in the eye. Then you say *'skål'* (pronounced *'skoal'*), take a sip, and then look the person right back in the eye again before setting down your glass (no clinking of glasses) and continuing your conversation. Eye contact is vital, and it is considered rude if it's not made, although foreigners can be excused. At dinner parties, you are also expected to make eye contact with everyone at the table who's seated near you, or is taking part in the *skål*.

Vinmonopolet stores are open from 10am to 5pm Monday to Wednesday, until 6pm Thursday and Friday, and until 3pm on Saturdays.

TO HELP YOU ORDER...

May we have a table? **Har du et bord?**
I'd like a/an/some... **Jeg vil gjerne ha...**
The bill, please... **Kan jeg få regningen?**

appetisers **forretter**	milk **melk**
bread **brød**	open sandwich **smørbrød**
butter **smør**	salad **salat**
coffee **kaffe**	soft drinks **brus**
cream **fløte**	tea **te**
fish **fisk**	vegetables **grønnsaker**
mains **hovedretter**	water **vann**
meat **kjøtt**	wine **vin**
menu **meny**	

...AND READ THE MENU

blåskjell mussels	**makrell** mackerel
dampet steamed/poached	**ost** cheese
eple apple	**ovenstekt** roasted
gravlaks marinated salmon	**pølse** sausage
grillet grilled	**reker** shrimp
gulrot carrot	**rosenkål** brussel sprouts
hvitløk garlic	**røktlaks** smoked salmon
jordbær strawberries	**sjampinjong/sopp**
kalv veal	mushrooms
kokt boiled	**skaldyr** shellfish
koteletter chops	**skinke** ham
krabbe crab	**stekt** fried
kylling chicken	**svinekjøtt** pork
kål cabbage	**torsk** cod
laks salmon	**tunfisk** tuna

PLACES TO EAT

Price ranges below are meant only as a rough guide to the price of a three-course meal per person with wine and tax included:

$$$$** over NOK 750   **$$$ NOK 500–750
$$** NOK 250–500   **$ less than NOK 250

CITY CENTRE

Annen Etage $$$ *Stortingsgata 24–26, tel: 21 54 79 70,* www.restauranteik.no. This restaurant directly above Theatercaféen in the Hotel Continental (its name means 'second floor') used to be among Oslo's most elegant, complete with a Michelin star. Now it is fairly dark and much less formal, with menu-based fare that means diners can only choose which courses they want, but it has quickly established itself as a trendy place to go in the city centre. It was opened by the chef behind the popular Restaurant Eik (see page 108). The bar offers 70 types of whisky. Closed during summer.

D/S Louise Restaurant & Bar $$ *Stranden 3, tel: 22 83 00 60,* www.dslouise.no. Maritime fans will love this place, inside the lively Aker Brygge waterfront complex. It is packed with an amazing assortment of nautical antiques and memorabilia from the glory days of transatlantic liner shipping. Ship horns ring every hour. The menu is also nostalgic, serving the kind of classic dishes that might have been found on board the old vessels, along with a solid assortment of seafood items.

Engebret Café $$$ *Bankplassen 1, tel: 22 82 25 25,* http://engebret-cafe.no. Engebret bills itself as Oslo's oldest restaurant – it has been serving continuously since the 1700s. It is indeed a historic place, with low ceilings and traditional Norwegian fare, featuring wild game during the autumn and lutefisk during the holiday season. You can dine outside from spring onwards, until autumn and winter drives everyone indoors. Check out the old-fashioned meeting rooms on the second floor.

Feinschmecker $$$$ *Balchens Gate 5*, tel: 22 12 93 80, www.
feinschmecker.no. State-of-the-art cooking is only half the story
at this, one of Oslo's finest restaurants. The cooking may push
new boundaries and have prices to match, but the atmosphere
is unpretentious and surprisingly welcoming. Seafood, international inflections and old Norwegian traditions all appear on a
seasonal menu with à la carte and set menu options. They have an
outstanding wine list.

Café Hemma Hos $$ *Fredrikborgsveien 16*, tel: 22 55 62 26, www.
cafehemmahos.no. If you are spending the day rambling around
the museums on the Bygdøy peninsula, plan your day around
lunch at this appealing modern eatery close to the Viking Ship
Museum. Salads, seafood and a series of set menus put a priority
on fresh tastes and the garden tables provide the perfect setting.

Kaffistova $ *Rosenkrantz Gate 8*, tel: 23 21 42 10, www.kaffistova.
com. This popular, cafeteria-style eatery is a bit of an institution in
Oslo, best-known for its traditional Norwegian country cooking
at reasonable prices. It is popular with visitors and city residents
alike, not least singles in need of a hearty, home-style meal with
none of the embarrassment they might otherwise feel when din-
ing alone. Super casual and steeped in Norwegian tradition, it is
located just off the lobby of the refurbished Hotel Bondeheimen.

Lorry $$ *Parkveien 12*, tel: 22 69 69 04, www.lorry.no. This is what
the Norwegians call a classic 'brown' establishment: down-to-
earth, folksy and serving traditional Scandinavian fare. It nonetheless has a touch of class, and waiters bustle around in black bow
ties and vests. Known for its choice of more than 100 types of beer,
the menu is varied, with both lighter meals like a seafood salad, a
relatively inexpensive 'dinner of the day' and a full à la carte offering. Most people come for the atmosphere, though.

Plah $$$ *Hegdehaugsveien 22*, tel: 22 56 43 00, www.plah.no. Plah
is billed as a gourmet Thai restaurant, sited just down a pedestrian
street from Lorry, and near the park around the Royal Palace. It
hit the Oslo scene with a bang and the entire Royal Family has
been known to assemble there for a relatively casual meal. The

food is creative and astonishingly good, and Plah is a great retreat on chilly Norwegian evenings.

Posthallen $$ *Prinsens Gate 8, tel: 22 42 82 00,* www.posthallen. no. Oslo's former main post office has been transformed into a mix of small apartments, shops, salons and this classy restaurant. The building, built in 1908, is full of new life and the food and atmosphere at Posthallen make for a unique dining experience. There may even be a show or exhibition going on in an open area near the tables.

Restaurant Eik $$$ *Universitetsgata 11, tel: 22 36 07 10,* www. restauranteik.no. One of the most popular restaurants in town, Eik pioneered the concept of menu-based fare, featuring the best ingredients of the season with wines to match. The food is gourmet-style without gourmet prices and Eik consistently wins rave reviews in local newspapers.

Rust $$$ *Hegehaugsveien 22, tel: 23 62 65 05,* www.rustoslo.com. Rust is the essence of the new Oslo – casual, classy and very cool with an international menu that ranges from tapas and salads to Asian-inspired dishes. When the weather is warm, the outdoor tables are the place to be, on a pedestrianised stretch of street up behind the Royal Palace.

Solsiden $$$ *Søndre Akershus Kai 34, tel: 22 33 36 30,* www.sol siden.no. You can't dine any closer to the water than at Solsiden, which translates as 'the sunny side' of the inner harbour. The restaurant's location inside a former waterfront warehouse makes it difficult to heat in the winter, so it's only open from May to September, and crowds flock there while they can. Solsiden has arguably the best fresh seafood in Oslo, prepared by cooks working from a raised, open kitchen running the length of the airy main dining room. Prices continue to rise here, but most still think it is worth it for a festive, summery meal.

Café Skansen $$$ *Rådhusgaten 32, tel: 24 20 13 11,* www.cafe skansen.no. This delightful, classic café opened in the summer of 2008 but seems like it has been at its historic location near the

Akershus Fortress forever. It serves Scandinavian fare, has popular outdoor tables in the summer and is modern yet traditionally cosy at the same time indoors. Its location makes it perfect for lunch or dinner during a busy day of sightseeing.

Statholdergaarden $$$$ *Rådhusgata 11, tel: 22 41 88 00*, www.statholdergaarden.no. Chef Bent Stiansen has been holding court here since winning the Bocuse d'Or in the early 1990s, and fans keep coming back for more. The building itself, a historic mansion dating back to the 1700s, is worth a visit. The food has secured Michelin stars for several years in a row. The restaurant on the second floor is an elegant establishment, while the much less formal 'kro' in the cellar (**Statholdergaardens Krostue $$$**) is easier on the wallet and reflects its owners' Danish influence. It is also open for lunch.

Taste of China $ *Torggata 18, tel: 22 11 18 88*, www.tasteofchina.no. Dim sum lovers welcomed the addition of this modest Cantonese-style restaurant, located in a colourful, crowded city-centre neighbourhood. They don't serve the dim sum from rolling carts like they do in Hong Kong, but the dim sum itself is delicious, easy to order from a menu with pictures of the food, and reasonably priced by Oslo standards. So is the beer and wine.

Theatercaféen $$$$ *Stortingsgata 24–26, tel: 22 82 40 50*. If you can only go out for one special dinner while in Oslo, this is the place to go. Theatercaféen is a landmark in the Norwegian capital, and one of the last authentic Viennese-style cafés in Northern Europe. The high ceilings, sketches of Norwegian artists, formally dressed waiters and live violin music streaming down from the balcony all contribute to the atmosphere. The food is good too, if pricey. This is the place 'to see and be seen' in Oslo. Government ministers, actors, musicians and local celebrities will likely surround you, even if you don't recognise them. Be sure to have some coins handy for the attendants in the toilets.

Ylajali $$$$$ *St Olavs Gate 2, tel: 22 20 64 86*, www.ylajali.no. Named after a character in the Hamsun novel Sult (Hunger), this cosy restaurant in a late-1800s building will clearly satisfy yours.

Ylajali (roughly pronounced '*Eee-la-ya-lee*') is one of several mid-range dining establishments to offer a 'menu-based' concept. You are told what's available, and then you choose how many courses you want. The food is consistently creative and good, and the service and surroundings are of a high yet informal standard. A thoroughly comfortable place to enjoy a solid meal in an old-fashioned setting.

OUTSIDE THE CITY CENTRE

EAST OF THE CENTRE

Ekeberg Restaurant $$$ *Kongsveien 15*, tel: 23 24 23 00, www.ekebergrestauranten.com. Eating at Ekeberg affords the diner what many consider to be the best view over the city and the fjord. The building, a classic, whitewashed example of early functional architecture from the early part of last century, was refurbished and reopened after years of neglect. It was an instant hit, offering outdoor dining and drinks and various menus inside. Its food, ranging from casual lunch dishes to gourmet dinners, has received mostly positive reviews. It's located just up the hill from the old seafarers' school, where you'll also find some ancient rock drawings.

Oslo Spiseforretning $$$ *Oslo Gate 15*, tel: 22 62 62 10, www.oslo-spiseforretning.no. The name roughly translates as 'the eating business', and that is what diners can do here in true Norwegian style. Oslo Spiseforretning only serves food made with Norwegian ingredients, and only meats from well-treated animals. It is a restaurant with a conscience, and located in the oldest part of town near the remnants of Viking and medieval settlements. The No. 18 and 19 trams heading for Ljabru stop near the front door.

SüdØst $$$ *Trondheimsveien 5*, tel: 23 35 30 70, www.sydost.no. The blazing fireplaces and open kitchen in this cavernous building in Grünerløkka are especially inviting on cold autumn and winter days. Outdoor seating along the Aker River makes SüdØst popular in the spring and summer, too. The food is wonderful, styled as Asian Crossover cuisine. The restaurant turns into a busy bar late at night. It also houses a bakery and café during the day.

Victor $$$ *Grefsenveien 6, tel: 22 22 17 70*, www.restaurantvictor. no. The à la carte menu changes here every week, but there's always a fish of the day and a five-course set menu. Restaurant Victor opened in an unlikely working-class neighbourhood in the mid-1990s and has inspired others to do the same. The feel of the place is French, and casually smart. The No. 11, 12 and 13 trams run by the front door.

FROGNER

Alex Sushi $$$$ *Cort Adelers Gate 2, tel: 22 43 99 99*, alexsushi. no. Some international reviewers have ranked this place as among the best sushi restaurants in the world, so be prepared for a fabulous, if expensive, experience. The key is the ultra-fresh Norwegian seafood, as well as some exotic imports and creative sushi concoctions. In addition to sitting around the sushi bar and watching master chefs in action, you can also sit at café-style tables and order menus that include such rarities as fresh whale and Norwegian lobster. Alex Sushi is almost always packed in the evenings, making reservations imperative, but it also opens for lunch and even offers high-class takeaway.

Bagatelle $$$$ *Bygdøy Allé 3, tel: 22 12 14 40*, www.bagatelle. no. Once known as Oslo's top restaurant, Bagatelle is under new management, with a new chef. They have a hard act to live up to, with Bagatelle's history of Michelin stars, exquisite service and gourmet menus. Time will tell.

Mares $$$ *Frognerveien 12, tel: 22 54 89 80*, www.mares.no. Many consider this to be the best seafood restaurant in town, and that is less debatable when Solsiden closes for the season. It's a small, minimalist place tucked into a vintage building in the fashionable Frogner neighbourhood. Servers have been known to sit down at the table with you to help you decide on a meal and choose a wine. Informal yet elegant, it's not cheap but offers good value for money by Oslo standards.

Palace Grill $$$ *Solligata 2, tel: 23 13 11 40*, palacegrill.no. Eating dinner at the tiny Palace Grill is more an experience than just a meal. It is important to come early if you hope to get a table, because no reservations are taken and it's always full. Adjoining a rowdy bar, the rough but cosy dining room attracts lots of men, not least because diners need a lot of capacity to fully appreciate the 11 different courses presented every evening. Patrons are expected to just sit back and let the expert waiters bring on the food, explain each course and suggest appropriate wines. This is not the place for picky eaters, or anyone with dietary restrictions.

MAJORSTUEN

Bambus $ *Kirkeveien 57, tel: 22 85 07 00*, www.bambussushi. no. This is a stylish, reasonably priced Asian restaurant with an interesting cross between Vietnamese, Thai and Japanese dishes, although sushi dominates proceedings. The woman running the place is stunningly elegant and firmly in command, but greets guests with a warmth not often found this far north. Bambus also has a comfortable bar area, where guests can enjoy small dishes, or pick up takeaway. Reservations are recommended, because the place is always busy.

Krishnas Cuisine $ *Kirkeveien 59B, tel: 22 60 62 50*, www. krishnas-cuisine.no. This is one of the few purely vegetarian restaurants in Oslo, and is found at one of the busiest intersections in town, in the upmarket Majorstuen district. The restaurant itself is unpretentious, on the second floor of a rather dull building. Three-course meals consist of the day's special, plus soup, salad, bread and rice; dishes include potatoes and vegetables in a sour-cream sauce and bean soup.

NORDMARKA

De Fem Stuer $$$$$ *Kongeveien 26, tel: 22 92 20 00*. You can't find more Norwegian romanticism than here in the main restaurant inside the fairytale-like Holmenkollen Park Hotel. This historic timber lodge is perched high above the city, and De Fem Stuer ('The Five Rooms') is full of elegant landscape oil paintings and antiques. The pricey menu offers Norwegian specialities in a traditional atmosphere. The view over the city is pretty nice too.

Grefsenkollen $$$$$ *Grefsenkollveien, tel: 22 15 70 33, www. grefsenkollen.no.* Escape the city for lunch or dinner at this 1926 timber lodge, which sits high on a hill, atop one of Oslo's best viewpoints. Grefsenkollen has a series of set gourmet menus. It caters to companies and groups but was open to the public at time of writing from Thursday through Saturday. The taxi fare adds to the high prices, but the excursion is worth it.

FURTHER AFIELD

Bølgen & Moi $$$$ *Sonja Henies Vei 31, Høvikodden, tel: 67 52 10 20, www.bolgenogmoi.no.* Spend an afternoon at the art museum created by Norwegian ice-skating star Sonja Henie, and after you've also seen all her trophies, and maybe even strolled around the museum's beautiful waterfront location on the fjord west of Oslo, head into this café and restaurant for a first-class meal. Bølgen & Moi was the first of chef Trond Moi's casual gourmet restaurants (there's another one in Oslo's Majorstuen district), and it is worth the drive out of town. The green suburban bus line also stops nearby: take the No. 261, 151 or 152 to Høvikodden. The café is open for lunch and dinner, serving creative dishes with the best ingredients Norway has to offer. Outdoor dining on the water is available when weather allows. The museum and restaurant are closed on Mondays.

Værtshuset Bærums Verk $$$$ *Vertshusveien 10, Bærums Verk, tel: 67 80 02 00, english.vaertshusetbaerum.no.* This restaurant could set the standard for Norwegian cosiness and they claim to be the oldest restaurant in Norway. It is situated in a centuries-old timber house in historic Bærums Verk, a former industrial village about half an hour's drive west of Oslo. The village itself is well worth a visit, with shops, galleries and a park-like setting along a rushing river. You can have dinner at the Værtshus, or local inn. The food is gourmet-quality with Norwegian tradition. The only disadvantage is the expensive taxi or long bus ride back to town.

A–Z TRAVEL TIPS

A Summary of Practical Information

A

ACCOMMODATION

Norway may be one of the most expensive countries on earth but hotel prices in Oslo are roughly on par with other major European cities. The vast majority of hotels are three or four-star, clean and inviting but with few frills like mini-bars or room service. There are several deluxe hotels in town that cater to business travellers. Most hotels offer attractive rates on weekends and during the summer.

Hotel rates in Oslo and most Norwegian cities actually *fall* from mid-June until mid-August. The local hotel market mostly caters to domestic business travellers and conferences, which dry up in the summer. Norwegians also tend to holiday at their own cabins or stay with friends and family in the cities. Hotels can be quiet at this time of year, and it is entirely possible to get a fine double room for around NOK 900 per night or less, even on weekends. Room rates always include taxes and breakfast.

Many of the hotel chains (like Rica and Thon) are domestic or operate only within Scandinavia or the Nordic countries. Several also offer a so-called 'hotel pass' for a modest fee. The passes provide reduced rates at all the properties in the chain, and some offer a free night's lodging after a certain number of nights. Fjord Pass (www.fjord-pass.com) is another useful scheme offering discounted rooms around the country for a one-off NOK 150 joining fee.

Oslo has some excellent B&Bs and a handful of pensjonat (pensions). In addition to those listed in this book, it is worth checking out www.bbnorway.com.

The Oslo Visitors' Bureau (www.visitoslo.com) can help arrange accommodation, but advance reservations are always a good idea. Quite a few accommodation links can be found on the bureau's website. English is widely spoken in Norwegian hotels.

AIRPORTS

Oslo Lufthavn **Gardermoen** (OSL; tel 91 50 64 00, www.osl.
no), is the capital's main international airport, about 50km (30
miles) northeast of the centre, with good public transport links
between the two. Most major airlines use Gardermoen, including
such carriers as SAS, British Airways, KLM, Air France, Continental, Finnair, Lufthansa, Aeroflot, Icelandair, LOT Polish Airways,
Norwegian Air and SN Brussels Airlines. Some budget carriers
like Ryanair use the airport at Sandefjord (called **Torp**) and list
it as 'Oslo', but it's a two-hour car or bus ride south-west of town,
longer in traffic.

The Airport Express Train (*Flytoget*) is the fastest connection between city and airport (half hour journey), but buses, local trains and
taxis are also available (one hour journey).

B

BICYCLE HIRE

Cycling is a popular means of transport in Oslo, and bikes are available to hire for exploring the city or the forests around town. Tomm
Murstad's Skiservice AS rents mountain bikes from its base just off
the Frognerseteren T-bane line at Voksenkollen (tel: 22 13 95 00). For
biking around the city, you can use the Oslo Bysykkel Scheme from
around Easter to late November (not available during the winter
because of snow and ice). A modest fee (around NOK 100) allows
you to unlock a bike from any one of nearly 100 bike stands around
town. Day passes are available for visitors. For more information,
consult the tourist information office or www.oslobysykkel.no (also
see page 92).

BUDGETING FOR YOUR TRIP

Oslo is one of the world's most expensive cities. Here is a sample of
average prices on essential services:

Airport transfer. The Airport Express Train (*Flytoget*; www.fly toget.no) is the fastest (about 30 minutes) and most popular means of getting into town, but it isn't cheap at NOK 170 for a one-way ticket. The local trains are slightly less, and fares vary depending on time of day. There are several airport bus lines, along with the hotel bus transfers. They take about an hour and cost around NOK 120. The taxi ride into town can cost more than a budget air fare to Oslo: as much as NOK 750 unless the taxi is ordered in advance, which makes the fare slightly cheaper. Enquire at the taxi desk inside the arrivals terminal.

The Oslo Pass. This discount pass is sold at hotels and tourist in-formation centres. It gives free travel on public transport , free ad-mission to many museums and sights, free parking at municipal car parks, and discounts on sightseeing tours, car rental, and at some shops and restaurants. The Pass is sold for 24, 48 and 72-hour periods and costs from NOK 270 to 495. See www.visitoslo.com.

Public transport. The city bus, tram and T-bane (metro) lines are all run by the same transit authority (Oslo Sporveier). The fare struc-ture can seem complicated. Single-fare tickets are good for an hour and honoured on all lines. Tickets can be bought from bus and tram drivers for NOK 50 onboard or for NOK 30 from a machine, a ticket booth at some tram stations, or a local kiosk.

Hotels. A dorm bed in a youth hostel will usually cost at least NOK350. Most local hotels are in the three-star range, and a nice double room with breakfast and all taxes can be found for around NOK 900 a night in the summer and at weekends (see Accommoda-tion). A night in a top hotel will cost around NOK 2,500.

Meals and drinks. A three-course evening meal at a mid-range res-taurant will usually cost at least NOK500. Beer is usually sold by the half-litre and costs about NOK 60. A glass of wine will run anywhere from NOK 60 to 100, bottles NOK 350–450 or higher. Cocktails are around NOK 120. Blame it on Norway's punitively high taxes on alcohol. This all means that a nice but relatively modest dinner for two will likely cost around NOK 1,000, more at upmarket establishments.

Museums. Admission to most museums and art galleries will rarely cost less than NOK50 and can go as high as NOK 120.

Entertainment. The standard movie ticket for an adult is NOK 100. Tickets to the theatre, ballet or opera usually cost NOK 250–450, lower than many other European or American cities, due to state subsidies.

Guided tours. There are many guided tour companies in Oslo that offer bus and boat rides. Most cost between NOK 350 and 450 and last about four hours.

C

CAMPING

Oslo is one of the few European capitals where camping is a real option, with the great outdoors less than 20 minutes from the city centre. Norwegian law allows camping anywhere in the forests, as long as you stay at least 150m (164yds) away from the nearest house or fenced property. There are three main camping grounds in Oslo, and regular bus lines into town serve all of them. Prices vary for tents, motor homes and trailers:

Ekeberg Camping (Ekebergveien 65; tel: 22 19 85 68; www.ekebergcamping.no). Ekeberg, a large plateau on a hill just east of the city centre, offers panoramic views over the city and down the fjord.

Bogstad Camping (Ankerveien 117; tel: 22 51 08 00; www.bogstadcamping.no). This classic camping ground is located just across the road from the exclusive Bogstad Golf Club and near Bogstad Lake, a popular recreational area on Oslo's northwest side.

Oslo Fjord Camping (Ljansbrukveien 1; tel: 22 75 20 55). Located on the grounds of a former manor house from the 1700s, near the popular Hvervenbukta Beach, on Oslo's southeast side.

CAR HIRE (See also Driving)

Narrow streets and parking challenges make having a car in the city centre a hassle. However, they are an advantage for excursions out of town. Expect to pay around NOK 1,200 a day for a medium-sized car, although it can be cheaper if you book in advance. There is rarely any real difference in price between local and international companies. Automatic transmissions are rare, so be prepared to shift gears.

Avis (tel 81 56 30 44; www.avis.no)

Bislet Bilutleie (tel 22 60 00 00; www.bislet.no)

Europcar (tel 67 16 58 30; www.europcar.no)

Hertz (tel 67 16 80 00; www.hertz.no)

SixT (tel 81 52 24 66; www.sixt.no)

CLIMATE

Oslo has four very distinct seasons, and while Norway is often associated with snow and ice, the city's winters are milder than one might expect. November is probably the least attractive month, because the days are short and the weather can be downright gloomy, with dark, rainy days. Many claim the best time to visit is in the summer, when the sun doesn't set until late in the evening and rises again by 4.30am. Oslo can be a summer paradise when the weather is nice, but there's no guarantee that this will be the case, and some summers are cool and rainy. Spring really bursts out all over, and April and May are festive months as the days grow noticeably longer. Autumn can be spectacular, with colourful foliage in and around town. Snow covers the ground from late November until April, although global warming seems to be changing all that.

	J	F	M	A	M	J	J	A	S	O	N	D
°C	−7	−7	−2	3	10	14	16	14	10	5	−1	−5
°F	19	19	28	37	50	57	61	57	50	41	30	23

CLOTHING

The unpredictable weather means preparing for just about anything. Walking is the best way to get around town, so sturdy walking shoes are important. Bring rain gear along from March to November. If visiting in the autumn or winter, you will need gloves, boots and a warm coat (although winter temperatures in Oslo rarely go below -10°C/14°F). In the summer, temperatures may reach 30°C (86°F), but 18–22°C (64–72°F) is the usual range, so dress accordingly. Oslo is a casual city, but many people dress up for dinner and a night on the town.

CRIME AND SAFETY (See Also Emergencies and Police)

Like many cities, Oslo has its share of robberies and violence, with much of the latter tied to drunken brawls and occurring late at night after the bars close. The city has been targeted by organised pick-pocket gangs in recent summers, so hang on securely to your wallets and purses, not least in hotel breakfast rooms, where some of the pickpockets have been caught operating. Beggars and prostitutes, many of them coming to affluent Norway from abroad, have also become a nuisance. However, most visitors experience no problems.

D

DRIVING

Rules and regulations. Norway generally follows Continental European driving regulations and uses the standard international road signs. There are some major things to remember, though:

Norway has a 'zero tolerance' policy regarding drinking and driving.

Drive on the right-hand side of the road; overtake on the left. Norway takes its 'right of way' rules seriously. Unless you are on a road or street featuring signs along the way with yellow triangles, you must give way to any car entering from the right. This applies even when it seems like you are on a main road and a car is entering from a minor side street. Motorists are not allowed to make right-hand turns at a red traffic light, even if no other cars are coming.

The speed limit is generally 50kmh (30mph) within the city limits and 80kmh (50mph) on highways, but follow posted speed limit signs. Speeding tickets are very expensive in Norway, and speed cameras are widespread.

Seat belts are mandatory front and back, and motorists must also drive with their headlights on at all times. The lights come on automatically on most Norwegian-registered cars when you start the ignition.

It is illegal to let a parked car idle, so turn off the engine if you want to avoid a ticket. It is also illegal to use a mobile telephone without a hands-free adaptor.

There are many toll roads (*bomvei*) in Norway, and motorists also must pay a toll (*bompenger*) to drive into Oslo. Most rental cars are equipped with an automatic subscription (*abonnement*) device mounted on the windscreen that allows the car to drive through toll stations lanes without stopping.

Pay attention to the unique Norwegian road signs warning of moose (*elg*) crossings. Some of the worst, fatal car accidents involve collisions with these huge animals.

For roadside assistance, call your hire company's emergency number or tel 08505.

Parking. Street parking in Oslo is generally pay and display. Parking may be free after 5pm on weekdays, 3pm on Saturdays and all day Sunday, so check the nearby signs.

Petrol stations in Norway are all self-service. Fill up first before paying at the counter inside the store. The price of unleaded petrol was around NOK 13 to NOK 14 per litre at the time of writing.

Are we on the right road for…? **Er dette riktig vei til…?**
My car has broken down. **Jeg har motorstopp.**
There's been an accident. **Vi har hatt en ulykke.**

E

ELECTRICITY

Norway uses standard two-pronged European plugs. The voltage is 220V.

EMBASSIES

Australia: The Australian Embassy in Denmark handles enquiries from Norway, Dampfaergevej 26, 2nd Floor, Copenhagen Ø, tel: +45 7026 3676, www.denmark.embassy.gov.au

Canada: Wergelands Vei 7, tel: 22 99 53 00, www.canadainternational.gc.ca/norway-norvege

Ireland: Haakon VIIs Gate 1, 5th floor, tel: 22 01 72 00, www.embassyofireland.no

New Zealand: The New Zealand Embassy in the Netherlands handles enquires from Norway, Eisenhowerlaan 77N, 2517 KK The Hague, +31 70 346 9324, www.nzembassy.com

South Africa: Drammensveien 88C, tel: 23 27 32 20; www.dirco.gov.za/oslo

UK: Thomas Heftyes Gate 8, tel: 23 13 27 00, ukinnorway.fco.gov.uk

US: Henrik Ibsens Gate 48, tel: 22 44 85 50, www.usa.no

EMERGENCIES

Fire: **110**
Police: **112**
Ambulance: **113**

G

GAY AND LESBIAN TRAVELLERS

Oslo is a fairly gay-friendly city, with some openly gay politicians. The annual Gay Pride parade on the third weekend of June attracts large crowds, and gay members of the Oslo police force may even march along in uniform. The event has been expanded into a week of revelry and special events called *Skeive dager*, *Gay and Lesbian Pride Week*, which includes the Oslo Gay and Lesbian Film Festival.

There are many gay bars and cafés in Oslo, featuring a mixed crowd of men and women. LLH is the main gay rights group in Norway: www.llh.no/english.

GETTING TO OSLO (See Also Airports)

By air. Several major airlines fly in and out of Oslo, but the most dominant carrier is Scandinavian Airlines (SAS), which is a member of the Star Alliance group. Other major carriers serving the main airport at Gardermoen include Aeroflot, Lufthansa, British Airways, KLM, Air France, Continental, Finnair, Icelandair and Norwegian. Ryanair flies into the Torp airport at Sandefjord, about a two-hour drive south of Oslo.

By sea. The most scenic way to approach Oslo is to sail up the fjord. Cruise-ferry lines have daily routes from Denmark (DFDS Seaways from Copenhagen, for example, www.dfds.com, and Stena, www.stenaline.no) and from Germany (Color Line, www.colorline.com, from Kiel). Color Line runs a fast-ferry from the northern tip of Denmark to Larvik, a two-hour drive south from Oslo.

By rail. From Oslo's central station you can catch a train to Copenhagen via Gothenburg and to Stockholm.

By road. The E6 and E18 highways are the main routes into Oslo from Sweden to the east and south. A bus service is available from Stockholm, Gothenburg and points in between. Among the major bus lines are Nor-Way Bussekspress (www.nor-way.no) and Swebus (www.swebusexpress.se).

GUIDES AND TOURS

There is a growing number of tour-guide companies in Oslo, including traditional bus tours and individually tailored tours for small groups. Guideservice AS (www.guideservice.no) and Oslo Guide Bureau (www.osloguide.no) are agencies that offer a mix of services. Among the major sightseeing tours are those run by HMK (www. hmk.no) and Oslo Sightseeing (www.boatsightseeing.com). There are also walking and boat tours, some with stands along the waterfront on the inner harbour. See www.visitoslo.com.

H

HEALTH AND MEDICAL CARE

The state-run health-care system is restricted to residents, except for emergencies. It is a good precaution to take out private health insurance, although EU residents can obtain reciprocal privileges with a European Health Insurance Card. There are also private clinics and emergency health-care centres, where English is widely spoken. Pharmacies (apotek) are scattered around town. Grocery and convenience stores sell painrelievers like paracetamol and ibuprofen (kept behind the counter).

24-hour pharmacy: Vitus Apotek, Jernbanetorget 4, tel: 23 35 81 00

HOLIDAYS

Banks, government offices and most businesses, including shops, are closed on the following holidays:

1 January New Year's Day **Nyttår**
March–April Maundy Thursday **Skjærtorsdag**
March–April Good Friday **Langfredag**
March–April Easter Monday **Annen påskedag**
1 May Labour Day **Første mai**
17 May Constitution Day **Grunnlovsdag**
May Ascension Day **Kristi himmelfartsdag**
May–June Whit Monday **Annen pinsedag**
25 December Christmas Day **Første Juledag**
26 December Boxing Day

L

LANGUAGE

Norwegian is one of the three Scandinavian languages and is North Germanic in origin, sharing similarities with Danish and Swedish. There are two official forms of Norwegian, *bokmål* and *nynorsk*. The former reflects Norway's 400 years of Danish domination, its more conservative form of *riksmål* even more so, while *nynorsk* is built on native Norwegian dialects, and is more prevalent outside Oslo and in southern Norway. Use of the two languages is subject to great political debate, and there have been attempts to remove *nynorsk* as a required subject in Oslo schools, all unsuccessful to date. Norwegians can choose to receive official papers, such as tax forms, in either *bokmål* or *nynorsk*. The Norwegian alphabet contains 29 letters, the standard 'a' to 'z' plus the vowels 'æ, ø' and 'å'.

The vast majority of Norwegians speak and understand English, and many are conversant in several other languages as well.

Some everyday phrases (with a guide to pronunciation):

hello **hei/goddag** *goo dog*

goodbye **farvel/ha det** *ha deh*

good evening **god kveld** *goo-kveld*

good night **god natt, natta** *goo-naht*

How are you? **Hvordan står det til?** *voor-dawn store deh till*

Pleased to meet you. **Hyggelig å treffe deg**. *hygg-a-lee oh treff-ah die*

Do you speak English? **Snakker du engelsk?** *snah-ker do ehng-elsk*

I don't speak Norwegian. **Jeg snakker ikke norsk**. *yigh snah-ker ick-keh norsk*

I don't understand. **Jeg forstår ikke**. *yigh fore-store ick-keh*

My name is... **Mitt navn er...** *mit nah-vehn are*

What time is it? **Hvor mye er klokken?** *voor me-yah are clock-en*

yes/no **ja/nei** *ya/nigh*
thank you **takk, tusen takk** *tock, too-zen tock*
no thank you **nei takk** *nigh tock*
excuse me **unnskyld** *ewn-schul*

Days of the week:
Monday **mandag**
Tuesday **tirsdag**
Wednesday **onsdag**
Thursday **torsdag**
Friday **fredag**
Saturday **lørdag**
Sunday **søndag**

Directions:
left **til venstre**
right **til høyre**
straight **rett frem**
back **tilbake**

Numbers:
1 **en**
2 **to**
3 **tre**
4 **fire ('fee-ruh')**
5 **fem**
6 **seks**
7 **sju ('shoe')**
8 **åtte**
9 **ni**
10 **ti**
100 **hundre**
1,000 **tusen**

M

MEDIA

Most major international newspapers can be found in Oslo, including the *Financial Times, International Herald Tribune, USA Today* and the *Wall Street Journal Europe*, along with most European dailies. For local news, try Aftenposten (www.aftenposten.no) or Dagbladet (www.dagbladet.no).

MONEY

Norway's currency is the krone (plural: kroner), or 'crown', and is represented by the abbreviations 'kr.' or NOK. Banknotes come in 50, 100, 200, 500 and 1,000 denominations, with the 200-kroner note now the most prevalent. There are also 1, 5, 10 and 20 kroner coins. One krone consists of 100 øre.

Currency exchange. There are minibanks (ATMs) all over town, but better exchange rates can be found at the Forex offices in Oslo, part of the Swedish currency-exchange firm. Banks and post offices also exchange money.

Credit cards. These are accepted just about everywhere, and are the most common form of payment, along with debit cards.

O

OPENING TIMES

Shops. Opening hours remain subject to some government regulation, but the rules have been relaxed considerably. Shops are open from 9 or 10am until 5 or 6pm, later on Thursdays. Stores in shopping centres usually remain open until 8pm. Many grocery shops are open until 9 or 10pm. Most shops close by 3 or 4pm on Saturdays, unless they are in a shopping centre that stays open later. Nearly everything is closed on Sunday, except on weekends in December. Convenience shops like 7-Eleven are open around the clock, as are some kiosks.

Banks. Open 9am–5pm. May have shorter hours in summer.
Office hours. Usually 9am–4pm, Monday to Friday.

P

POLICE (See also Crime and Safety)

The regular Norwegian police *(politi)* force is unarmed and officers are friendly and approachable. There is a police station in the main Oslo S train station, among other locations. Oslo also has a mounted police force, with horse stables near the landmark Akershus Fortress and Castle.

POST OFFICES

Many post offices in Norway have closed or been replaced with postal counters inside grocery stores in some towns. In Oslo, there are still a number of post offices scattered about town. Most are open from 9am (some earlier) until 5pm, and until 3pm on Saturdays. Post offices also function as banks, and offer currency exchange along with various products for sale, such as stationery.

T

TELEPHONE

There are still a few phone booths in Oslo, but the classic red ones are now considered historic monuments.

To call a number in Oslo from abroad, dial your international access code (00 in Europe, 011 in the US, for example) and then the country code for Norway (47) and the eight-digit number, which in Oslo usually begins with 22. To call within Norway, simply dial the eight-digit number. Most mobile phone numbers begin with a 9, but some start with a 4.

Mobile coverage is excellent around the country. Roaming is possible as long as you're carrying a GSM, dual- or tri-band cellular phone. Local SIM cards can be purchased from 7-Eleven and Narvesen convenience stores, although the instructions may be in Norwegian. Otherwise, try a Telehuset outlet.

TIME ZONES

Norway is in the European time zone, one hour ahead of Greenwich time. Daylight-saving time takes effect from the last Sunday in March to the last Sunday in October, like most of the rest of Europe. The following is a chart of summer times:

New York	London	**Oslo**	Jo'burg	Sydney
6am	11am	**noon**	noon	8pm

TIPPING

Restaurants include a service charge in the bill, but it has become customary to also leave a tip. A 10 percent tip is generous and recommended only when service has been exceptional. Most Norwegians round up the bill, or leave 5–10 percent in cash on the table. Increasingly, restaurants are using portable credit card terminals, where the customer is expected to include a tip when punching in the total amount to be billed, while the server discreetly looks away.

Taxi drivers expect tips, but 10 percent is generous. Not many hotels have porters any more, but NOK 30 should be sufficient for those that do.

TOILETS

Toilets are either called 'WC' or 'Toalettet', with 'Herrer' for the men and 'Damer' for the women. There aren't many public toilets in Oslo, but they can be found in hotels, restaurants, cafés, museums and some shops. The classic old Theatre Café is known for its attendants in the toilets, who make small talk, tidy up constantly and offer hand towels, all for a small fee. Have a NOK 10 coin handy.

TOURIST INFORMATION

The main tourist information office (tel 81 53 05 55; www.visitoslo.com; daily May–Sept 9am–6pm, Oct–Apr Mon–Fri 9am–5pm, 9am–4pm Sat–Sun) is located near the city-side entrance of the City Hall, at Fridtjof Nansens Plass 5. There is also a tourist information office in the central railway station. Most hotels have vast racks of brochures and maps, and front-desk staff are often helpful.

Norwegian embassies around the world offer lots of current information, including details of cultural events in Norway. To find an embassy in your area, visit www.norway.info. The Norwegian Embassy in Washington, DC, is particularly helpful: www.norway.org. The government website www.norway.no is full of information for foreigners in Norway.

TRANSPORT

Oslo's public transport is expensive, extensive and reliable, with a vast network of bus, tram, ferry, T-bane (metro) and suburban rail lines. The websites www.trafikanten.no and ruter.no offer journey planning, and there are free maps of the network at tourist information counters, hotels and in countless brochures.

In general, Oslo's public transport system operates with a standard one-trip fare with pricing by zone, but there are also 24-hour tickets, which are often cheaper. The same tickets can be used on the tram, T-bane and the red city bus, but not the green suburban bus system.

Taxis. Deregulation of the taxi system has led to a proliferation of new taxi companies, if not lower fares. It will cost at least NOK 100 even for short trips, while most are in the NOK 150 range. One consolation is that taxis tend to be quite nice, usually new luxury cars like Mercedes or Volvo. There are taxi stands all over town, and you can also flag them down on the street. Available taxis will have an illuminated sign on the roof. The pricing system is similar to most other cities in the world with a flagfall (from NOK 50) and a rate per km or minute, which varies depending on the time of day.

Where can I get a taxi? **Hvor kan jeg finne en drosje/ taxiholdeplass?**

What is the fare to...? **Hvor mye koster det å kjøre til...?**

Where is the nearest bus stop? **Hvor er narmeste bussholdeplass?**

When is the next bus to...? **Når går neste buss til... ?**

I want a ticket to... **Jeg vil gjerne ha en billett til...**

single/return **en vei/tur-retur**

Will you tell me when to get off? **Kan du fortelle meg når jeg skal gå av?**

V

VISAS AND ENTRY REQUIREMENTS

Passports/Visas. All citizens of the European Union, the Nordic countries, the US, Canada, Australia and New Zealand can enter Norway without a visa and stay for up to 90 days, as can citizens from many other countries. For details, see the Immigration Directorate's website, www.udi.no. Norway is part of the 'Schengen' passport-free area, so arrivals from most European airports won't encounter any passport control at Oslo's airport. Those arriving directly from outside Schengen (including Ireland, Switzerland, the UK and the US) will need to present their passports.

W

WEBSITES AND INTERNET ACCESS

There are WiFi zones throughout town. Look for WiFi signs in windows.

Visit Oslo (www.visitoslo.com) The tourist office site and easily the best.

Visit Norway (www.visitnorway.com) Good overview of Oslo.

Norway Guide (www.norwayguide.no) Good information on Oslo.

Use-It Oslo (www.use-it.no) Youth information: shopping, nightlife, activities etc…

Norway Post (www.norwaypost.no) English-language news about Norway.

Y

YOUTH HOSTELS

Oslo is an expensive city, but it is not impossible to get a reasonably priced place to stay. Norske Vandrerhjem (tel 23 12 45 10; hihostels. no) is the country's official youth hostelling association.

Anker Hostel (Storgata 55; tel: 22 99 72 00; www.ankerhostel. no) is close to the popular Grünerløkka district and offers a hotel-type room or four- to six-bed rooms. There are plans to open a larger, affiliated hostel further north in Grünerløkka. Rates per person.

Perminalen Hotel in the heart of the city (Øvre Slottsgate 2; tel: 23 09 30 81; www.perminalen.no) has been catering to students and young adults for years. Rates by the bed.

There are two other hostels in the Oslo area, the **Oslo Vandrerhjem at Haraldsheim** (Haraldsheimveien 4; tel: 22 22 29 65; www.haraldsheim.no), located 4km (2½ miles) from the city centre in the Grefsen area, and **Oslo Vandrerhjem Holtekilen** (Michelets Vei 55, 1368 Stabekk; tel: 67 51 80 40; www.hihostels.no), just west of Oslo in the suburban township of Bærum. Private and shared rooms, plus meals.

One of the most unusual budget places to stay in Oslo is on board an old passenger ship moored on the eastern side of Akershus Fortress, the **MS *Innvik*** (tel: 22 41 95 00). Single and double cabins with breakfast.

Recommended Hotels

Most of Oslo's hotels reflect the Norwegian mentality that built the country's social welfare state: nothing should be too fancy or too basic. Most of the accommodation on offer in Oslo is of a high standard, clean and comfortable, although differences do, of course, exist. Hotel rates tend to be around the same as in many other European capitals, which is surprising considering the high prices of just about everything else in town. Most hotels include a buffet breakfast and taxes in their rates.

High occupancy levels have spurred construction of some new hotels, including the recent expansion of airport hotels. Some will be built in outlying areas, but most hotels remain concentrated in the city centre or on the fringe of the centre in the Frogner and Majorstuen neighbourhoods.

The symbols below reflect standard rates based on double occupancy with breakfast and taxes included. Single room rates are usually NOK 200 or NOK 100 lower, and many hotels also offer lower rates on weekends and in the summer.

$$$$	over NOK 1,800
$$$	NOK 1,200–1,800
$$	NOK 900–1,200
$	NOK 450–900

CITY CENTRE

Hotel Bondeheimen $$ *Rosenkrantz Gate 8, tel: 23 21 41 00,* www. bondeheimen.com *or* www.bestwestern.com. Owned by a group that promotes Norwegian agriculture, Hotel Bondeheimen is like a piece of rural Norway plopped down in the middle of the city. Its name literally translates to 'farmers' home'. This is where people from the country traditionally stayed while in the capital. Its popular cafeteria-style restaurant still specialises in Norwegian country cooking, and there is also a traditional craft shop on the ground floor. The 127-room hotel is part of the Best Western international hotel chain, but local traditions persist. Hot soup, bread and butter are served in the lobby on weekday afternoons as an extra gesture of country hospitality.

Bristol $$$ *Kristian IVs Gate 7, tel: 22 82 60 00,* www.thonhotels.no/bristol. The Hotel Bristol is an institution in Oslo, with its extravagant lobby, Bristol Grill restaurant and Library Bar, where journalists can often be seen interviewing local celebrities. The hotel dates from the 1920s and has been beautifully preserved, with few signs of its ownership by the large, otherwise mid-level Thon Hotels group. The Bristol consistently gets good reviews. It is located a block from Karl Johans Gate and the Parliament building in the heart of the city.

Cochs Pensjonat $ *Parkveien 25, entrance around the corner on Hegdehaugsveien, tel: 23 33 24 00,* www.cochspensjonat.no. This is a popular hostelry in a classic five-storey residential building from the turn of the last century. It has been a lodging establishment for more than 75 years and has a long literary history, even playing a role in the 2005 Norwegian novel *The Half Brother*, which won the Nordic Council's literature prize. Its 88 rooms vary in standard and price; some even have a kitchenette. Cochs is located just behind the park surrounding the Royal Palace.

Continental $$$$ *Stortingsgata 24–26, tel: 22 82 40 00,* www.hotel-continental.no. One of Oslo's top hotels, the family-owned and operated Continental also appears in lists of the best hotels in Northern Europe. The Continental has 154 rooms, of which 23 are suites, and is located in the heart of town across from the National Theatre. The hotel is home to the famous Theatercaféen and a sedate lobby bar called Dagligstuen, which is also frequented by local celebrities. This is a hotel for executives, or those celebrating a special occasion.

Ellingsens Pensjonat $ *Holtegata 25, tel: 22 60 03 59,* ellingsenspensjonat.no. This friendly little guesthouse occupies a late 19th century building and traces of that era still remain, not least in the high ceilings in most rooms. Rooms are simple but impeccably maintained with fresh flowers on the windowsills, pristine white walls and comfortable beds. Most have refrigerators and a kettle for making coffee and tea. The guesthouse is just northwest of the centre, around 500m/yds northwest of the Royal Palace's parkland, off Hegdehaugsveien. It is a 20-minute walk downtown, but is uphill all the way back. It is wonderfully quiet at night.

Grand Hotel $$$$ *Karl Johans Gate 31, tel: 23 21 22 00*, www.grand. no. This is where the winner of the Nobel Peace Prize stays, and it is arguably the grandest establishment in town. The Grand has a long history in Oslo and a prime location, just across the street from the Parliament. Its elegant Grand Café on the street level was a favourite haunt of playwright Henrik Ibsen, who is featured in the café's murals and has a hotel suite named after him. The Grand has nearly 300 rooms, a special floor dedicated to women, and a number of restaurants.

Grims Grenka $$$ *Kongens Gate 5, tel: 23 10 72 00*, www.firsthotels. com. This so-called 'design hotel without the attitude' finally opened in 2008 after months of delays. It is part of the First Hotels chain and boasts 'exotic Norwegian design' at its location in Kvadraturen, the historic grid behind Akershus Fortress. The area is being steadily revitalised with galleries, restaurants and even museums opening up, but caution is advised on the streets at night. Once inside, the hotel sports an ultra-modern lobby and atrium, various bars and an Asian crossover restaurant.

Karl Johan Hotel $$$ *Karl Johans Gate 33, tel: 23 16 17 00*, www. karljohan.no. This stylish place is located in the heart of town, next door to the Grand Hotel and across from the park-like mall that runs from the Parliament to the National Theatre. Most of its rooms are spacious and well appointed, but late-night party animals on the streets below may bother some guests. The hotel is now part of the Best Western group of hotels.

P-Hotel $ *Grensen 19, tel: 80 04 68 35*, www.p-hotels.com. You could not be much more central than at this hotel, which lies just a block northeast of Karl Johans gate. The comfortable, but no-frills rooms are outstanding value, especially given the location, and some come with carpet, others parquet or hardwood floors. They keep costs down here by keeping unnecessary services to a minimum – for example, breakfast is included, but is delivered to your room in a bag every morning. You can also make your own tea or coffee in the rooms.

Perminalen Hotel $ *Øvre Slottsgate 2, tel: 24 00 55 00,* www.permi nalen.no. This basic hotel near the Parliament appeals to young people on a tight budget. It offers simple rooms with a bath; it's possible to pay just for a bed in a four-bunk room.

Radisson Blu Plaza Hotel $$$$ *Sonja Henies Plass 3, tel: 22 05 80 00,* www.radissonblu.com/plazahotel-oslo. Former US president Bill Clinton stayed here, as have countless other dignitaries and rock stars. This modernistic high-rise, unusual for Oslo, is located adjacent to the Oslo Spektrum arena, and just across the street from the central train station (Oslo S). The immediate surroundings are heavily trafficked, but the views from rooms on high floors can't be beaten. There's also a restaurant and bar at the top of the hotel, reachable by an outdoor elevator to the 34th floor.

Radisson Blu Scandinavia Hotel $$$ *Holbergs Gate 30, tel: 23 29 30 00,* www.radissonblu.com/scandinaviahotel-oslo. This was one of the first semi-highrises built in Oslo, and it still stands out as it towers alone over a neighbourhood near the park around the Royal Palace. It is a classic SAS business hotel, not especially warm or cosy, but pure Scandinavian in its clean lines and no-nonsense style. There is a popular bar on the top floor.

Rica Victoria Hotel $$$ *Rosenkrantzgata 13, tel: 24 14 70 00,* www. rica.no. Tourists can be seen lining up outside this hotel to board a bus all summer long, but there is a reason it is popular with tour groups as well as independent travellers. It is an ideal base for exploring the city, located between Karl Johans Gate and the City Hall's large plaza (Rådhusplassen) on the waterfront at the inner harbour. The hotel is modern and proud of its lunch buffets. Night-time noise can be a problem on weekends.

Hotel Savoy $$$ *Universitetsgata 11, tel: 23 35 42 00,* www.choice hotels.no. The Savoy has been completely renovated and now sports one of the hottest restaurants in town, Restaurant Eik, on its ground floor. Its 93 rooms and lobby are now ultra-modern and minimalist in style. It is located next door to the National Gallery and surrounded by several top antique stores and other galleries.

Vika Atrium Hotel $$$ *Munkedamsveien 45, tel: 22 83 33 00,* www.thonhotels.no. This is another hotel ideally located for exploring the city, sitting right behind the popular Aker Brygge waterfront complex of shops and restaurants. Some rooms have views to the inner harbour area, and most major sights are within walking distance. The hotel, situated inside a mirrored-glass office building and conference centre, is part of the mid-priced Thon Hotels group, which offers favourable summer and weekend rates and incentive programmes for staying at other Thon Hotels in Norway.

OUTSIDE THE CITY CENTRE

Hotel Gabelshus $$$ *Gabels Gate 16, tel: 23 27 65 00,* www.choice hotels.no. A relatively recent renovation radically altered this gracious old hostelry, originally a villa built in 1912 in the heart of the embassy district of Frogner/Skillebekk. Gabelshus was connected to another elderly hotel located directly behind it, the former Ritz, and today their 114 rooms are rather chic and trendy. Gabelshus is quiet and comfortable, with a spa on the premises.

Kampen Hotel $$ *Kjølberg Gate 29, tel: 24 07 40 00,* www.kampen hotell.com *or* www.bestwestern.com. Initially intended as an apartment complex, the developers of this hotel instead opted to turn it into a hotel with rooms of varying sizes and all with full kitchen and balcony. It is the only hotel in this part of eastern Oslo at Tøyen, close to the Munch Museum, Botanical Gardens and the historic neighbourhood of Kampen.

Radisson SAS Hotel Nydalen $$$ *Nydalsveien 33, tel: 23 26 30 00,* www.radissonblu.com/hotelnydalen-oslo. This was the first hotel to be built outside the city centre in some time. It is located in a former industrial area along the Aker River, and was built in conjunction with offices, flats and a business college. It only takes around 15 minutes to get into the city centre, though, thanks to a T-bane line to the Nydalen area. The hotel is part of the Radisson chain, modern in style, and with views over the city and fjord.

Rica Hotel Bygdøy Allé $$ *Bygdøy Allé 53, tel: 23 08 58 00, www. rica.no.* An elaborate building from days gone by houses this hotel, which is part of the Rica chain and has long been a fixture in the fashionable Frogner district, home to nearly all of Norway's foreign embassies. The hotel is a short walk from Frogner Park and about a half an hour's walk down stylish Bygdøy Allé into town, unless you want to hop on the red city bus that drives by all day long.

West Hotel $$ *Skovveien 15, tel: 23 27 64 64, www.bestwestern.no.* The West Hotel is located on a fashionable shopping street behind the Royal Palace. The hotel's bar and restaurant have long been popular gathering places for residents of the Frogner neighbourhood, even though the restaurant's management and style have changed often. The hotel has 56 rooms, eight of which have balconies, and it's part of the Best Western chain.

NORDMARKA

Holmenkollen Park Hotel $$$$ *Kongeveien 26, tel: 22 92 20 00, www.holmenkollenparkhotel.no.* This fairy-tale-like timber hotel is in a class of its own, and can be seen from all over town because of its hillside perch. The Holmenkollen is a romantic establishment from 100 years ago, floodlit at night and full of Norwegian antiques and oil paintings. The rooms, though, are in a modern wing adjacent to the original timber structure, and many have sweeping views over the city, fjord and adjacent forests. It takes half an hour to get into town on the T-bane line, which stops nearby. Holmenkollen really is a destination in itself.

Lysebu $$$$ *Lysebuveien 12, tel: 21 51 10 00, www.lysebu.no.* Lysebu is owned by a foundation that seeks to foster ties between Denmark and Norway and is mostly used as a conference venue, though it has lately nurtured a role in the regular hotel trade. The location is lovely, in the hills above Oslo with hiking and cycling trails at the front door. It is also close to the Tryvann ski centre, and relishes its perch on the fringe of the forest known as Nordmarka. This is a top-class, elegant retreat, with charming rooms and two dining rooms affording panoramic views.

Losby Gods $$$ *Losbyveien 270, 1475 Finstadjordet, tel: 67 92 33 00*, www.losbygods.no. It is best to have a car to get here, but it will be worth the journey. Losby Gods is only about half an hour's drive from the city centre, but is a world away, nestled on the northern fringe of the eastern hills and forest of Østmarka. The hotel is of modern construction, but built in the same style as the gracious old manor house from the mid-1800s that was the heart of Losby's 'gods', or estate. The rooms are first-class, the dining room serves fine meals, and the hotel is surrounded by a golf course, and hiking and cycling trails that double as ski trails in the winter. An overnight stay at Losby could easily be combined with an excursion to Eidsvoll.

Radisson SAS Airport Hotel $$$ *Hotelvegen, Gardermoen, tel: 63 93 30 00*, www.radissonblu.com/hotel-osloairport. This stylish, modern hotel is located just a five-minute walk from the terminal at Oslo's main airport at Gardermoen. Booming business prompted a major expansion after just seven years of operation, and travellers can't beat its convenience. Some dignitaries and executives fly in and hold their meetings here, without even making the trip into central Oslo. It's a smart place to stay for those with early-morning flights.

Refsnes Gods $$$ *Godset 5, 1518 Moss, tel: 69 27 83 00*, www.dehistoriske.com/hotel/refsnes-gods or www.refsnesgods.com. If you drive south to Drøbak or beyond, Refsnes Gods makes a nice place to stay overnight. It is part of a chain of historic hotels in Norway that offer top-rate food and lodging. The hotel, originally built as a twin-towered summer home in 1767, is located right on the Oslo Fjord on the island called Jeløy, just outside Moss. The hotel has a swimming pool and sauna, and there is a well-known art gallery nearby.

INDEX

Berlitz pocket guide

Oslo

Third Edition 2014

Written by Nina Kay Berglund
Updated by Anthony Ham
Edited by Tom Stainer
Art Editor: Shahid Mahmood
Series Editor: Tom Stainer
Production: Tynan Dean and Rebeka Ellam

Photography credits: All Glyn Genin/Apa Publications except; Scala 2/3M, 62; Alamy 40, 60/61 68, 75, 78/79; Anna Mockford and Nick Bonnetti/Apa Publications 2TL, 4ML, 5MC, 4/5T, 6ML, 7MC, 7MC, 15, 16/17, 28/29, 38, 39, 42/43, 56, 96/97, 98, 99; AWL Images 26; Getty 2/3M, 23, 54, 76/77, 80, 90/91; Hadeland Glassworks 5TC; Innovation Norway 74; iStockphoto 4MR, 64/65, 70/71, 72/73, 100, 102; Norway Says 7TC, 66; Norwegian Center for Design Architecture 67

Cover picture: Bigstockphoto

Printed in China by CTPS

Berlitz Trademark Reg. U.S. Patent Office and other countries. Marca Registrada. Used under licence from the Berlitz Investment Corporation

Every effort has been made to provide accurate information in this publication, but changes are inevitable. The publisher cannot be responsible for any resulting loss, inconvenience or injury.

Contact us

At Berlitz we strive to keep our guides as accurate and up to date as possible, but if you find anything that has changed, or if you have any suggestions on ways to improve this guide, then we would be delighted to hear from you.

Berlitz Publishing, PO Box 7910,
London SE1 1WE, England.
email: berlitz@apaguide.co.uk
www.insightguides.com/berlitz

T-bane Metro

Frognerseteren

1

- Frognerseteren
- Voksenkollen
- Lillevann
- Skogen
- Voksenlia
- Holmenkollen
- Besserud
- Midtstuen
- Skådalen
- Vettakollen
- Gulleråsen
- Gråkammen
- Slemdal
- Ris
- Gaustad
- Vinde
- Steinerud
- Frøen

T-bane Metro

━━━ Kun mandag–fredag 07–19
Monday–Friday 07–19 only

► Gulleråsen: Stopp bare i pilretningen
Gulleråsen: Stop in direction of arrow only

Forbindelser Connections

🚢 Tog
Railway

🚌 Bussterminal, region- eller fjernbusser
Bus terminal, regional or long distance services

12 Trikkelinje
Tram line

20 Høyfrekvent bybusslinje
High frequency city bus line

30 301 Andre utvalgte busslinjer
Other selected bus lines

Ekraveien · Røa · Hovseter · Holmen · Makrellbekken · Smestad · Bor

23

32
Eiksmarka

Lijordet

Østerås

5

Østerås

23
- Montebello
- Ullernåser
- Åsjordet
- Bjørnsletta
- **13** Jar
- Ringstabek
- **142 143** Bekkestua
- Gjønnes

2

Gjønnes

Under ombygging,
Kolsås 2014
Under reconstruction,
Kolsås 2014

Kolsås

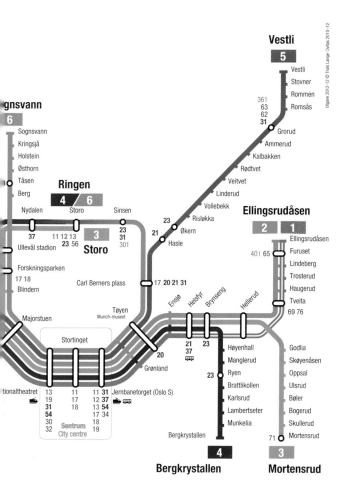

Vestli

5

Vestli
Stovner
Rommen
Romsås

361
63
62
31
Grorud
Ammerud
Kalbakken
Rødtvet
Veitvet
Linderud
Vollebekk
Ellingrudåsen
Risløkka
2 **1**
23
21 Økern
Ellingrudåsen
401 65 Furuset
Hasle
Lindeberg
Trosterud
Haugerud
Tveita
69 76

gnsvann

6

Sognsvann
Kringsjå
Holstein
Østhorn
Tåsen
Ringen
Berg

4 / 6

Nydalen Storo Sinsen

37
23
11 12 13 **31**
23 56 **3** 301
Ullevål stadion
Storo

Forskningsparken

17 18
Carl Berners plass 17 **20 21 31**

Blindern

Ensjø Helsfyr Brynseng Hellerud
Tøyen
Munch-museet
Majorstuen

Stortinget

21
37 23
🚌

Grønland 20 Høyenhall Godlia

23 Ryen Skøyenåsen
Manglerud
Oppsal
Brattlikollen
Ulsrud
tionaltheatret 13 11 11 **31** Jernbanetorget (Oslo S) Karlsrud Bøler
🚢 19 17 12 **37** 🚢 🚌 Lambertseter Bogerud
31 18 13 **54** Munkelia Skullerud
54 17 34 71 Mortensrud
30 18
32 **Sentrum** 19 Bergkrystallen
City centre

4 **3**

Bergkrystallen **Mortensrud**

Utgave 2012-12 © Trafs Lange Oxilas 2010-12

 **Berlitz**®

speaking your language

phrase book & dictionary
phrase book & CD

Available in: Arabic, Cantonese Chinese, Croatian, Czech, Danish, Dutch, English*, Finnish*, French, German, Greek, Hebrew*, Hindi, Hungarian*, Indonesian, Italian, Japanese, Korean, Latin American Spanish, Mandarin Chinese, Mexican Spanish, Norwegian, Polish, Portuguese, Romanian*, Russian, Spanish, Swedish, Thai, Turkish, Vietnamese

*Book only

www.berlitzpublishing.com